Dr. Lawrence M.F. Sudbury, PhD

NICEA:
WHAT IT WAS,
WHAT IT WAS NOT

(c) Lawrence M.F. Sudbury
All Rights Reserved

13 Digit ISBN 978-0-9790625-2-0
10 Digit ISBN 0-9790625-2-7

www.newburghseminary.com

Printed In The United States of America

To Silvana,
my mother and first teacher

Dr. Lawrence M.F. Sudbury – **Nicea: what it was, what it was not**

CONTENTS

PREMISE: THE NEED FOR A STUDY — p. 7

I - AN HISTORICAL BACKGROUND
I.1) THE EMPIRE BEFORE THE UPCOMING OF CONSTANTINE — p. 13
I.2) THE CHURCH BEFORE THE UPCOMING OF CONSTANTINE — p. 27
I.3) CONSTANTINE: HIS TIME, HIS EMPIRE, HIS CHURCH — p. 47

II - THE COUNCIL
II.1) A DIVIDED CHURCH, A DIVIDED EMPIRE — p. 69
II.2) THE CALL FOR NICEA — p. 83
II.3) WHAT WE HISTORICALLY KNOW — p. 91

III - THE DOCUMENTS
III.1) THE FINAL DOCUMENTS — p. 107
III.2) THE SYNODAL LETTER — p. 121
III.3) THE CANON, THE CHURCH AND THE CLERGY — p. 135
III.4) CONSTANTINE'S LETTERS — p. 153

IV - PERPLEXITIES AND MISTAKES
IV.1) WHERE IS THE CANON? — p. 165
IV.2) NICEA AFTER NICEA — p. 173
IV.3) CONCLUSIONS: QUESTIONS AND ANSWERS — p. 183

APPENDIX I:
THE CAPTIONS OF THE ARABIC CANONS ATTRIBUTED TO THE COUNCIL OF NICEA — p. 193

APPENDIX II:
BIBLIOGRAPHY — p. 201

SPECIAL THANKS — p. 209

Dr. Lawrence M.F. Sudbury – **Nicea: what it was, what it was not**

PREMISE: THE NEED FOR A STUDY

"Constantine needed to strengthen the new Christian tradition, and held a famous ecumenical gathering known as the council of Nicea...."
"At this gathering, many aspects of Christianity were debated and voted upon - the date of Easter, the role of the bishops, the administration of sacraments, and, of course, the divinity of Jesus."
"My dear, until that moment in history, Jesus was viewed by His followers as a mortal prophet... a great and powerful man, but a man nevertheless. A mortal."
"Jesus' establishment as 'the Son of God' was officially proposed and voted on by the council of Nicea... a relatively close vote at that."
"Establishing Christ's divinity was critical to the further unification of the Roman empire and to the new Vatican power base...."
"Constantine collated an entirely new Bible at the council of Nicea, containing only books that speak of Jesus as divine. All books that portrayed him as human were burned"[1].

These are just some of the statements contained in one of the most read books of last twenty years: that *The Da Vinci Code* by Dan Brown which, although being a declared novel, for a long time has influenced (and, somehow, is still influencing) the religious ideas of a big slice of its readers.

All the mentioned sentences are supposed to come from Sir Leigh Teabing, introduced in the book as a British Royal historian. But are we so sure his words really sound as documented certitudes and they are not just some sort of repeated historical rumors, constantly present in the most scandalmongering and inferior pseudo-historical post-Enlightenment productions?

On the other hand, let's have a look to this short "apolytikion troparion"[2] about the emperor Constantine, sung in Orthodox

---

1) D.Brown, *The Da Vinci Code*, Doubleday 2003, passim
2) A short dismissal hymn

Churches at the end of many functions of the Divine Liturgy:
"*He beheld the image of Your Cross in the Heavens and, as Paul, he too did not receive the call from men. Your Apostle among Kings placed the care of the Royal City in Your hands. Through the intercessions of the Theotokos, O only Loving Lord, keep it ever in peace.*"[3]

For Western believers, the mention inside of a Divine Liturgy of an Emperor who, according to the majority of the historians, along his life ordered to kill his eldest son Crispus and his wife Fausta, could seem at least a bit exaggerated and perhaps even blasphemous, but we don't have to forget that, for the Orthodox Church, Constantine the Great is "Saint Constantine", also nicknamed "the Thirteenth Apostle", one of the strongest defenders of the Church of all times and a "vessel of the Holy Spirit"[4]. Which are the elements defining, according to the Orthodox believers, Constantine a Saint? Dr. Demetrios Olufallidis, Academic of the Byzantine Patriarchate of Constantinople, after mentioning a number of miracles (from the well known vision of the cross before the Battle of the Milvian Bridge to a presumed recovery from leprosy, actually without any historical clue) having Constantine as protagonist, in relation to the Nicene council writes:

"*Saint Constantine, willing to save the Christianity from the diffused plague of the Arian Heresy, enlightened by the Holy Spirit, personally wrote to all the bishops of the known world and prayed them in the name of Christ, to join together to discuss about the future of the Holy Church. [...] He housed the delegates of all dioceses in his luxurious palace in Nicea, but he decided to reside in an humble cell of the local monastery, in continuous contemplation of the Holy Cross. [...] When, during the forth day of the council he spoke to all bishops, a legend says a dove could be seen behind his left shoulder and his words sounded to all the present venerable*

---

3) AA.VV., *The Jordanville Orthodox Prayer Book*, Holy Trinity Monastery 2003, p. 288

4) Constatine is defined with these terms in the "*Kontakion tou Agiou Costantinou*" another hymn of the Orthodox Church

holy men like coming directly from God. He explained to all the bishops that the true nature of Christ could be easily found in the Scriptures and that only Satan, through the mouth of his evil servants, like Arius, could deny what was plain to all hearts touched by the Divine Spirit of God. [...] After his speech no one could anymore dissent that the true was coming from his mouth and as one men all the presents voted to declare Arius a vile heretic"[5].

Even with the normal customary tare we must apply to the rhetoric and the rather low level of scientific nature of a XIX century strongly ideologically addressed writing, it is out of doubt that the role given to Constantine in the council of Nicea by the Orthodox Church still remains the one of an extreme pre-eminence. But, was Constantine really a protagonist of the council? Was he such an humble and blessed man as described in the just mentioned short passage?

Between the extremes of the two examples coming from a XXI century novel with some historical claims and a XIX century hagiography, literary hundreds of different assertions about what happened in Nicea can be found.

Some believe Nicea was the cradle of the Evangelical Canon the way we know it[6], some others think it was just a sort of farce whose decisions had already been taken much in advance by the imperial theologians[7], others are sure it was the first moment in which the divinity of Jesus was stated[8], others, finally, simply deny that it changed anything in the common notions of Christianity, just being an internal discussion about thin

---

5) D. Olufallidis, *Agiographies of the Most Important Saints of the Church*, Theotokos Publishing 1879, pp. 63-64
6) D.C. Parker, *The Living Text of the Gospels*, Cambridge University Press 1997, passim
7) B.D. Ehrman, *Lost Christianities: The Battles for Scripture and the Faiths We Never Knew*, Oxford University Press, 2005, pp. 187-195
8) R.E. Rubenstein, *When Jesus Became God: The Struggle to Define Christianity during the Last Days of Rome*, Harvest Books 2000, pp. 106-127

theological distinctions, absolutely unimportant for the common Christian believers[9]. And this just to mention a few examples of the most common ideas.

So, in such a puzzling scenario, where is the truth? What did the council deal with? Which were its decisions and statements? Which was the role of the Roman empire in its definitive assumptions?

Actually, we don't lack the sources to trace the historical roots of Nicea nor we lack testimonial documents about the proceeding of the debate held in the imperial palaces and about its results. Simply, the majority of the documents we have are subjective descriptions or partial testimonies and this is the element making the historical work quite difficult, involving the need for the interpretation of any report in the light of a re-contextualization of its meaning in its historical period .

A difficult task, for sure, but anyway possible, provided to have the will to overpass ideological or instrumental mental barriers and to try to use the scientific methods of the historical study, without the need to look for extraordinary or scandalmongering "truths".

Possibly this is the problem of many studies lately published. And it is also the reason to try, through a patient study of the chronicles of the time and of the writings of the many historians who faced the reconstruction of the council along the centuries, to draw an as objective as possible picture of what Nicea was and of what it was not.

---

9) L.C. Jackson, *Faith of Our Fathers: A Study of the Nicene Creed*, Canon Press 2007, passim

I

AN HISTORICAL BACKGROUND

Dr. Lawrence M.F. Sudbury – **Nicea: what it was, what it was not**

I.1) THE EMPIRE BEFORE THE UPCOMING OF CONSTANTINE

In order to understand the events moving to the call for the Nicean council, we must take things a little bit at large, first of all trying to analyze the situation of the Roman empire inherited by Constantine.
Generally, we refer to the long period inaugurated by the crowning of Commodus (A.D. 180) and ended in A.D. 476 with the deposition of Romolus Augustus by Odoacer as "the decline and fall" of the empire.
Actually this term is quite improper: on one hand, socially nothing really changed with the passage of the throne to Odoacer, as, finally, it had already been in the ends of almost barbarian emperors since centuries before, on the other end, the empire, meant as political institution, had already died much before, at the time of Diocletian, with the institution of the imperial quadrumvirate[10]. Since that moment on, we can really speak about a new era for Rome and, consequently, for the whole Western world still submitted by the imperial eagles, a new era in which Nicea had to become a new pillar of the "status quo". It is, therefore, necessary, if we want to understand the environment which will take to the council, to briefly analyze the period just starting from its very beginnings.
 Diocletian (A.D. 284-305) came to the throne after a century of disorganization, internal dissent, economic crisis, and foreign invasions.
The situation of the whole empire was close to the collapse. The population was decimated and demoralized. Many of the peasants had become serfs, tied to the soil for local lords in return for protection. Large sections of the empire's agriculture

---

10) D. Kagan, *The End of the Roman Empire: Decline or Transformation?*, D.C. Heath & Co. 1992, pp. 21-23

and trade were wrecked. The coinage was debased to the point of being almost worthless. The frontiers were under constant pressure. And the army was in serious need of reforms. Everywhere he looked Diocletian saw serious problems, while the means to solve those problems were horribly damaged. Being a tough and practical soldier he had one ambition: to retire from the imperiate alive. And he managed to do it (an exceptional feat) at the price of a radical breakdown of the imperial unity[11].

Unlike the previous soldier-emperors from the Danubian area Diocletian, born in an humble family of Salonae, in Dalmatia, had no outstanding gifts as a general[12], although he was a rather competent soldier. But he exhibited capability, or, at any rate, energy, such as was rarely found among later Roman emperors. It soon became clear that he had pondered over the problems of the empire and had plans ready to meet them.

He concentrated mainly on three issues: defense, creating a more efficient government, and protecting the emperor against revolts and assassination[13].

Turning to the army, Diocletian saw two needs that worked against each other: the need for efficient defense against the growing threats on his frontiers and the need for insurance against revolts. The larger the army he created, the more potential there was for revolt. But too small an army meant invasions, which was even worse. Therefore, he increased the army to twice its size under Augustus. And since there were now simultaneous threats on several frontiers, Diocletian also

---

11) G. Downey, *The Late Roman Empire*, Holt, Rinehart and Winston 1969, pp. 83-111
12) Actually his rise to the power had been probably due to his offices as freedman of the Senator Anulinus and, later, as chief of the Praetorians, the emperor's bodyguards and not to particular merits in any warfare campaign
13) S. Williams, *Diocletian and the Roman Recovery*, Routledge 1996, p.16

split this army into two parts: stationary frontier militia who could stop small invasions and slow down big ones, and mobile legions, increasingly made of cavalry, that could rush to any trouble spots that the militia could not handle.

Unfortunately, the Roman populace, unused to military service after the "Pax Romana" and reduced in numbers by the recent anarchy, could not provide the number and quality of recruits that were needed. As a result, the government resorted more and more to recruiting Germanic tribesmen who were willing to fight for Rome for a price. While these recruits were warlike enough, they were generally unwilling to submit to the level of discipline and training that had made the Roman army so effective through the centuries. As a result, the Roman army, especially in the West where roughly half the recruits were Germanic, decayed to a pathetic shell of its former greatness.

However, this larger army further increased the danger of revolts by powerful generals. Diocletian did three things to protect himself against this. First, he broke the army into smaller commands for each general, while keeping part of the mobile legions under his personal command. Second, he split the control of each province between civil and military authorities. This made it harder for a rebellious general to command such resources as food and money needed for a successful revolt. However, it also meant that civil governors and generals might not cooperate against invasions[14]. Finally, Diocletian isolated himself with elaborate court rituals similar to that of the Persians. Not only did this physically separate him from potential assassins, it also gave him a semi-divine status that made attacking the emperor seem like a sacrilege.

Also in relation to the government, a new start had to be made; no longer could one emperor sit at Rome and control the whole

---

14) M. J. Nicasie, *Twilight of Empire: The Roman Army from the Reign of Diocletian until the Battle of Adrianople*, J.C. Gieben1998, passim

web of interests of an enormous territory. An emperor had to be on the field wherever frontiers were threatened: the problem was that there were too many frontiers to control and that generals sent in peripheral territories instead of the supreme leader might be tempted to continue the dreary process of attempted usurpation.

So Diocletian decided to move his staff and court ("comitatus") to Milan, much closer to the risky Northern border[15] and, at the same time, to supplement his own efforts by appointing helpers of outstanding authority. Therefore, Diocletian split the empire between the Latin speaking West and the Greek speaking East, with an emperor, known as an Augustus, and separate administration in each half. Technically, there was still one Roman empire, but more and more it functioned as two independent and, at times, competing empires. Overall, splitting the empire aggravated the natural split between Greek East and Latin West and prevented cooperation when it was most needed[16].

Anyway, in A.D. 285 he named a Danubian compatriot, M. Aurelius Valerius Maximianus, as Caesar, and while he himself took the title "Jovius", he granted the name of "Herculius" to his co-regent. The two men would act together under the shield of their patron gods, the greater god being assigned to the greater ruler, while the humble origin of the two emperors might be forgotten in the gleam of this new celestial light[17].

In the following year Maximianus was given the rank of Augustus as a reward for his efficient crushing of a revolt in Gaul of wandering bands of discontented poor peasants named

---

15) In fact throughout his reign he visited Rome only once

16) E. Gibbon, *The Decline and Fall of the Roman Empire*, Phoenix Press 2005, pp.161-167

17) R. Rees, *Diocletian and the Tetrarchy*, Edinburgh University Press 2004, passim

"Bagaudae". Intermittently, for the next four or five years, Maximianus had to contend with attacks across the upper Rhine by Alamanni and Burgundi, while further North the Franks had to be continuously checked, until the moment in which, in A.D. 288, a Frankish chief accepted peace in return for the title of King of the Franks.

Maximianus was less successful in his attempt to clear the English Channel of Saxon and Frankish pirates, since a Messapian named M. Aurelius Mausaeus Carausius, whom he had appointed as commander of a fleet based at Gesoriacum (modern Boulogne), crushed the pirates but decided to use his naval power to proclaim himself "Augustus" and to occupy Britain, where, in A.D. 287, he set up a sort of small local empire.

During these years Diocletian was based at Nicomedia in Bithynia, from where he went to the Danube to defeat the Sarmatae (A.D.289 and A.D. 292), to Syria against Saracen invaders (A.D. 299), and to Egypt to crush a revolt of the native Blemmyes (A.D. 291). He also secured an Arsacid on the throne of Armenia without provoking Persia to war[18].

Although for many years Maximianus had played his part well, in A.D. 293 Diocletian carried the delegation of functions a stage further: one emperor could not be omnipresent, but four could cover more ground than two.

He therefore nominated two young officers, C. Flavius Valerius Constantius (4) (usually known as Constantius Chlorus), who was also of Illyrian-Danubian origin, and C. Galerius Valerius Maximianus, to a share of the imperial power.

While Diocletian and Maximianus were nominally joint emperors (like M. Aurelius and L. Verus had been, in completely different times, between A.D. 161 and A.D. 169) and shared the title of Augustus, Galerius and Constantius were named Caesars

---

18) M. J. Nicasie, *Cit.*, pp. 57-71

and became heirs-expectant to the two senior rulers.

The division of the competence between the four leaders was made on a territorial basis: Diocletian assigned Italy, Africa, Spain and the Northern frontier provinces to Maximianus, whose Caesar, Constantius, received Gaul and Britain, while he kept for himself the East and Egypt, assigning most of the Balkans to his Caesar, Galerius.

The primary object of establishing this quadrumvirate was undoubtedly military, but it was also intended to provide for an orderly succession. At first sight the plan might appear as a revival of the triumvirates which had hastened rather than retarded the fall of the Republic, yet under Diocletian's supervision it worked well. By virtue of his personal authority, the chief partner remained in effect the sole emperor, while he secured the loyal assistance of three of the best military commanders of the Roman army: Constantius, who had been praetorian prefect and had already married Maximianus' step-daughter (turning away Helena, the mother of Constantine) was a man of statesmanlike qualities, while, Galerius, who had divorced his wife in order to marry Diocletian's daughter Valeria, was a much harder man[19], even if the unflattering portrait drawn by some Christian writers of this persecutor of Christianity is probably exaggerated[20].

Although Diocletian's reign was not free from attempted usurpations, this new asset of power did not lead to any general recurrence of civil war.

Actually, in A.D. 296, an adventurer named L. Domitius Domitianus with a lieutenant named Achilleus assumed the imperial title in Alexandria, but he was promptly crushed by Diocletian in person.

---

19) R. Rees, *Cit.*, pp. 70-87
20) W. Leadbetter, *Galerius and the Will of Diocletian*, Routledge 2008, pp. 11-13

Much more serious was Carausius' claim to become a third Augustus: the whole Britain had escaped many of the troubles of the third century and Carausius had had time and wealth to organize the defense of the Eastern and Southern coasts of the island against the Saxons by building some of the so-called "Saxon Shore Forts". Probably the quadrumvirate was quite worried by his requests but just before having the possibility to negotiate with Diocletian, Carausius was murdered and supplanted by a subordinate named Allectus in A.D. 293. Allectus had much less appeal on the British population than Carausius and, already in A.D. 296, Constantius, the Caesar charged of the defence of Britannia, mounted an invasion against him. The war strategy adopted by the Caesar was very effective: while Constantius made a demonstration in the Channel, his praetorian prefect, Asclepiodotus, eluded the enemy fleet in a mist and landed near Southampton Water. He then defeated Allectus's army near Silchester, while Constantius' forces sailed up the River Thames just in time to save London from some of Allectus' defeated but marauding troops. Thus with the collapse of the "Imperium Britanniarum" the unity of the empire was restored[21].

In the absence of continuous civil wars Diocletian's colleagues were able to give a good account of themselves in frontier defense: Constantius (A.D. 297-298), crushed some invasions by the Alamanni in Gaul, Galerius kept order on the Danube, and Maximianus in A.D. 298 subdued the Quinquegetani, a Moorish tribe in Africa.

In the meanwhile, in A.D. 296 Diocletian was called upon to defend Mesopotamia, which had been ceded by the Persian king Bahram in 284: a new and vigorous king named Narses declared

---

21) J.C.S. Léon, *Los Bagaudas: Rebeldes, Demonios, Mártires. Revuelatas Campesinas in Galia y Hispania Durante el Bajo Imperio*, University of Jaén, 1996, pp. 93-116

war and Diocletian entrusted the conduct of this Persian war to Galerius, who, after an initial defeat at Carrhae, acted decently by transferring operations to Armenia, destroying Narses's army in a second battle and capturing Ctesiphon. Diocletian did not follow up on his lieutenant's success, but he restored Roman suzerainty and was apparently content to let the Roman frontier lie on the line from Nisbis to Singara, with control over the whole of the upper Tigris basin. The alliance with Armenia was subsequently strengthened by the conversion of its ruler Tiridates III (261-317) to Christianity, which definitely estranged him from the Sassanids, even if it did not draw him nearer to the Caesars.

With these operations the frontiers were made safe for the time being against major invasions, and an anxious period of forty years, in which crisis followed crisis, drew to a close: the "tetrarchy" (the official Greek name of the quadrumvirate) inaugurated by Diocletian appeared to have justified itself by its results[22].

Unfortunately, a larger army, bureaucracy, and elaborate court required heavy taxes. In order to ensure a stable tax base, people and their descendants were tied to their stations in life. Not only did a shoemaker, soldier, or farmer have to remain in his profession for life, but his sons had to follow in his footsteps, as did their sons after them and so on. This, plus the high taxes, reduced people's incentive to work hard and helped create a stagnant economy. The depressed economy meant a lower tax base to draw taxes from, which forced the government to further raise taxes, thus catching Roman society in a vicious feedback cycle, similar to the one that triggered the anarchy of the III century.

So, finally, the balance of Diocletian's reforms shows both shadows and light spots: the Roman empire under Diocletian

---

22) S. Williams, *Cit.*, pp. 116-121

presents a depressing picture, with its frontiers under constant pressure, oppressive taxes, and people stuck in their positions in society. However, it was more secure from invasion, which did allow trade and agriculture to revive somehow. One might doubt whether Roman security was worth the price paid for it. However, Diocletian did accomplish one thing of importance for later civilization. He propped the Roman empire back up for two more centuries, allowing the new tribes along the northern frontiers to become more accustomed to Roman civilization through trade, raiding its borders, and serving as mercenaries in its army. When the Western half of the empire finally fell by A.D. 500, these tribes were more willing to try to preserve Roman civilization and pass its heritage on to the Middle Ages and eventually to our own culture[23].

The real enormous problem of all the system was another: its success was due largely to the personal ascendancy of the emperor, for it was this and not the system itself that checked the ambitions of his colleagues[24].

But Diocletian was getting older and he was feeling the burden of rule, while in the early years of the new century he had to face, as we will see, the divisive aspect of Christianity in the empire and growing pressures from Galerius, willing to obtain the promised charge of Augustus.

Thus, in late A.D. 303 when he went with Maximianus to Rome to celebrate his twentieth anniversary as emperor he decided that both men should retire early in A.D. 305, after Maximianus had celebrated his "vicennalia" in turn, and he extracted an oath from his colleague to fulfill his promise.

On May 1st, A.D. 305, therefore, Diocletian formally abdicated at Nicomedia and Maximianus at Milan, and their Caesars, Galerius and Constantius, succeeded them as Augusti. But the

---

23) G. Downey, *Cit.*, pp. 147-149
24) R. Rees, *Cit.*, pp. 208-211

appointment of two new Caesars was less easy. On a dynastic principle the two obvious candidates were Maxentius, son of Maximianus, and Constantine, the illegitimate son of Constantius. The point is that Diocletian did not consider the former suitable and therefore thought it wiser to pass them both by. The new Caesars were Flavius Valerius Severus, an Illyrian friend of Galerius, in the West, and C. Galerius Valerius Maximinus Daia, Galerius' nephew, in the East.

By the territorial division which followed, Constantius held Britain, Gaul and Spain, and his Caesar, Severus, had Africa, Italy and Pannonia. Galerius received Asia Minor west of the Taurus Mountains, while Maximinus had the other Asiatic provinces and Egypt. Although theoretically Constantius was the senior Augustus, Galerius seemed to have obtained the best of the bargain, as through Severus he could control much of the West and, at the same time, put pressure on Constantius since he held his son Constantine at his own court. Under this arrangement the Roman empire was virtually partitioned into separate and rival sovereignties and Diocletian's retirement, an act theoretically of self-denial, ended in a sort of reshuffle of all roles with the result of breaking an already precarious balance[25].

While Diocletian contentedly cultivated vegetables[26] in his great palace at Salona (modern Split) and Maximianus reluctantly endured retirement in Lucania, the pattern of power changed rapidly. Constantius, who already had carried through some

---

25) M.P. Southern, *The Roman Empire from Severus to Constantine*, Routledge 2001, pp. 236-258

26) When, in June A.D.308, the situation of tensions among the various pretenders to the different positions of the tetrarchy became unbearable and practically an open civil war was going to destroy the new asset of Rome, some Roman emissaries of Galerius went, as we will see, to Diocletian, in his enormous palace in Salona, asking him to intervene and to take the "imperium" back he, unable to solve the problem and, perhaps, totally enslaved by the deep depression that hit him in the last years of his life, simply answered: "*I can't. I must crop the cabbages and the peas*".

reconstruction in Britain, was needed there again, either to punish or anticipate attacks by the Picts (Caledonians) in the North of the province. He seized this chance to ask Galerius to let his son Constantine join him for the campaign. Galerius could hardly refuse this request unless he was prepared for civil war. Constantine however, took no chances. He traveled by forced marches and killed the past-horses behind him, since even if Galerius took no direct action, traveling through Severus' territory might prove hazardous. However, he safely joined his father at Boulogne early in A.D. 306 and together they carried through a campaign which reached the North of Scotland. But after this victory Constantius died at York, and the army proclaimed Constantine as Augustus in his father's place. While waiting for Galerius' reply to a request for recognition, Constantine strengthened his position by leading his main army from Britain to Southern Gaul, where he learned that Galerius had compromised: Severus was to be the new Augustus, but Constantine was recognized as Caesar.

He gave in for the moment; civil war was averted and the tetrarchy was saved.

Constantine's success goaded Maximianus' son Maxentius, to become the figurehead, if not the spearhead, of a revolt in Rome caused by taxation and the suppression of the Praetorian Guard (October A.D. 306). This popular movement elevated Maxentius as Princeps (he avoided claiming any more provocative title); he was accepted by Southern Italy and Africa, but Northern Italy stood by Severus. Support of the Praetorians and urban cohorts would not carry him far, so he successfully appealed to his father Maximianus to come out of retirement to help him.

Galerius' reaction was to order Severus to march on Rome. But Maximianus resumed his title of Augustus and drove Severus back to Ravenna, where he was captured. Maxentius was proclaimed Augustus in A.D. 307. In order to face the expected counter-attack by Galerius, Maxentius sought the support of Constantine, whom he won over by giving him his sister Fausta in marriage and acknowledging him as Augustus in return for similar recognition. Galerius' invasion was not long delayed and he reached as far as Interamna without opposition. However, he lacked the means for an attack on Rome itself, his troops became disaffected and he was forced to retire, while Maxentius, curiously, made no effort to hamper his retreat. In the meantime Severus had been put to death in captivity. Maxentius next found himself double-crossed by his own father, who tried to persuade Constantine to come South in order to crush the retreating Galerius and then Maxentius. Constantine refused, although he broke off relations with Maxentius when he heard that Spain had declared for him. So the father was left to tackle his son alone. Late in A.D. 307 Maximianus went to Rome and after a few months of joint rule he tried to overthrow Maxentius, tearing his purple robe from him. But he misjudged the temper of the soldiers, who rallied to the son and forced Maximianus to flee to his son-in-law Constantine, leaving Maxentius in control of Rome (early A.D. 308). Galerius attempted a new settlement by appealing to the aged Diocletian to come out of his retreat and attend a conference at Carnuntum which Maximian also attended in November A.D. 308. Diocletian refused to get the purple back and persuaded his old colleague Maximianus to retire again. Galerius nominated an old companion in arms, Licinianus Licinius, to succeed Severus as junior Augustus with control of Italy, Africa and Spain (which in fact were held by Maxentius who was now declared a usurper); Maximinus continued as Caesar in the East, while Constantine was demoted in rank to Caesar of Gaul and Britain. The two Caesars refused to be placated by the title of "Sons of the Augusti", and so in A.D. 310 Galerius had to agree to their claim to be Augusti.

Thus, there were now four Augusti (Galerius, Licinius,

Constantine and Maximinus), while Maxentius was unrecognized, although he held Italy, Africa and Spain.

In A.D. 310 one major piece disappeared from the chess-board. Maximianus, who had returned to his son-in-law Constantine in Gaul, tried to win over some troops while Constantine was busy campaigning against the Franks. The coup failed and Constantine probably acquiesced in, if he did not order, his death. Thus, a link snapped between Constantine and the "Herculius" Augustus, who had first recognized him as Augustus, so Constantine began to look for a new basis for his authority. He propagated the idea that his father, Constantius, was descended from Claudius Gothicus and adopted the Unconquered Sun ("Sol Invictus") in place of Hercules as the patron of the dynasty.

Early in A.D. 311 Galerius died after an illness which he attributed to the God of the Christians whom he had mercilessly persecuted; a death-bed repentance resulted in an edict granting greater tolerance to Christians, but not in his recovery[27]. The four survivors played for position. Maximinus Daia overran Asia Minor before Licinius could, and then reached an agreement with him. Constantine, anticipating a struggle against Maxentius, made an agreement with Licinius (who was engaged to his sister Constantia), who, in turn, drove Maximinus into the arms of Maxentius in Italy[28].

---

27) W. Leadbetter, *Cit.*, pp. 298-302
28) The whole reconstruction of the period A.D. 306-310 is based on: T.D. Barnes, *The New Empire of Diocletian and Constantine*, Harvard University Press, 1982, pp. 186-223

Dr. Lawrence M.F. Sudbury – **Nicea: what it was, what it was not**

I.2) THE CHURCH BEFORE THE UPCOMING OF CONSTANTINE

Which was the role of the Church in all this troubled period? Which had been its evolution? As the roots of the subjects discussed in Nicea and of the role of the emperor in the council stand much before that A.D. 325 that saw the bishops join together to take decisions about the destiny of the Church, once again we must take things a bit at large, to clear some elements which will be useful later to a deeper understanding of the real themes of the Nicene council.

Since the end of the so-called apostolic period in the late first century, the question that dominated the various churches already created was that of understanding Jesus in and through the events of His ministry. Although in a variety of particular forms, the Christology of incarnation dominated the literature of the end of the first century and the beginning of the second. Ignatius, the bishop of Antioch, for whom Jesus the Christ is to be understood as *"our God"*[29], in example, polemicized against Docetism, the view that the fleshly, bodily side of Jesus is mere "appearance", but insisted that Christ was truly born, truly suffered, and was truly crucified[30]. For Ignatius, there are two dimensions of the person of Christ. In Jesus, spirit and flesh, divine and human, are at one. *"There is only one physician - of flesh, yet spiritual, born yet unbegotten, God enfleshed, genuine life in the midst of death, sprung from Mary as well as God"*[31].

Christologies of this incarnational form are actually present in many other writings from other sectors of the church. Another famous example in this sense is the document called "1 Clement", a letter from the Roman congregation to that at

---

29) Ignatius of Antioch, *Epistula ad Ephesios*, III.2
30) Ignatius of Antioch, *Epistula ad Smyrneans*, I.2
31) Ignatius of Antioch, *Epistula ad Ephesios*, VII.2

Corinth, which portrays Jesus as the reflection of God's splendor, the *"mirror of God's [...] transcendent face"*[32] and the *"scepter of God's majesty"*[33], while a somewhat later writing from Rome, *The Shepherd of Hermas*, combines the idea of *"the holy pre-existent Spirit which created the whole creation"*[34] with the picture of Jesus as the suffering and exalted servant[35].

In this period, more or less by A.D.100, Christianity was present in Asia Minor (the most Christianized territory), Syria, Macedonia, Greece and the city of Rome and, by A.D. 130, also in Egypt[36]. This is the time in which we can assist to the development of a body of literature traditionally referred to as the "Apostolic Fathers". In this "corpus" we can already find traces of a primitive dispute about the church leadership: again in *"1 Clement"*, written around A.D. 95 and, probably wrongly[37], attributed to Clement, a prominent presbyter of the Roman church, the author deals with problems of order in the face of a rebellion in Corinth against the authority of that presbyters of the Church, while again Ignatius of Antioch, in his seven letters (ca. A.D. 113), urges unity in Christ through obedient fellowship with the bishops, presbyters and deacons of the local church, and, in the process, argues against Docetic and Judaizing doctrines. A general survey of this literature makes clear that Christianity in the opening decades of the second century was beset by debate and conflict, but it also makes clear that the churches were working toward common solutions to these problems as also attested by their habit of writing each other

---

32) *1 Clement*, XXXVI
33) *1 Clement*, XVI.2
34) *Sheppard of Hermas, Similitudes*, V.6
35) W.Walker, *A History of the Christian Church*, Scribner 1985, pp.82-91
36) E.Ferguson, *Backgrounds of Early Christianity*, Wm. B. Eerdmans Publishing Company 1993, p.46
37) R.A. Whitacre, *A Patristic Reader*, Endrickson Publishers, 2007, p. 91

letters of rebuke, advice and exhortation[38].

In the meanwhile, the position of Rome towards this rapidly growing faith was quite ambivalent. In matters of religion, Rome was normally tolerant and permitted (and even, in some cases, protected) local or ethnic cults. Thus, Judaism was a "religio licita", an authorized religion. But, at the same time, Romans were traditionally wary of voluntary religious societies ("collegia") that practiced their rites in private. Members of such groups were likely to be suspected of taking blood oaths that pledged them to crime and sedition. For such a dangerous association, Christianity became a very likely candidate, since it was not a traditional religion and could not claim the same recognition as, for example, Judaism. What is more, Christians gathered in private and openly refused all participation in pagan religious observances. This marked them as not only being suspect, but also as dissenters in any "polis" where they dwelt[39]. Very often it was not imperial policy but popular hostility that instigated the early persecutions: at Lyons and Vienne in Gaul, in example, it was the rage of *"an infuriated populace against its supposed enemies and foes"*[40] which started the persecution in A.D.177[41]. The charges brought against the Christians caused the emergence of a new genre of Christian literature, the "apology", taken from the Greek "apologia", meaning "a speech for the defense". The authors of these writings, known collectively as "the Apologists", wrote their works mainly between A.D.130 and A.D.180 and what is interesting is to see that the majority of them didn't seem to be so afraid of the Roman power, but simply to try to expose and spread their

---

38) T.Dowley, *Introduction to the History of Christianity*, Augsburg Fortress Publishers, 1994, pp.45-66
39) An example of the suspects towards the Christians can be found in Pliny: Pliny, *Epistualae*, X.96
40) Eusebius, *Historia Ecclesiastica*, I, VIII
41) W.Walker, *Cit.*, pp.111ff

ideas[42]. Paradoxically, many Christian writers seemed to be much more engaged with groups which came to be called "Gnostics". As a result of this debate, the Church was compelled to significantly develop in the range, depth and precision of its theological tradition[43]. Yet, in spite of the significance of this debate, it is difficult now to clearly delineate the phenomenon of Gnosticism. The cultural and social setting of this movement was the urban world in which Jewish religious texts and symbols were being drawn into syncretism with popularized philosophical notions and themes drawn from Hellenistic religion.

It's not the case, here, to deepen the problem of Gnosticism. However, it is not by chance that the principal sources for knowledge of Gnosticism have been the works of its Christian opponents, late second and early third century writers such as Irenaeus of Lyons, Clement of Alexandria, Origen, Tertullian, and Hipplytus of Rome. From such writers two things become clear: first, Gnosticism was by no means a uniform phenomenon and there was no single body of teaching common to all. Second, it is clear that not all Gnosticism was Christian and that the movement existed independently of the Church, even if it did get from Christianity abundantly. However, one of the most common characteristics of Gnosticism was the offer of a secret teaching, the knowledge ("gnosis") of which could be grasped only by a selected few thanks to abstract philosophical or theological notions or religious symbols coming from different sources, as Gnosticism proved very syncretistic of Jewish scriptures, pagan mythology, popular astrology, magic, middle platonism, neo-pythagoreanism, and Hellenistic Judaism. Many Church fathers

---

42) A.R. Dulles, *A History of Apologetics*, Ignatius Press, 2005, passim
43) E.Ferguson, *Cit.*, pp. 86-94

traced Gnostic heresies back to Simon Magus in Samaria[44] but this artificial schematizing does fit the opinion of many modern scholars who see the real origin of Gnosticism in some intellectual circles in proximity to Judaism. There was, in fact, heavy contact of Gnosticism with Judaism before its contact with Christianity and any further contribution from the rest of the near East, so that the Gnosticism combated by the Church fathers, was surely mediated through Jewish channels. Nevertheless, many of the Gnostic texts found in Nag Hammadi in 1945 can be interpreted in a manner consistent with the Church fathers' view of Gnosticism as a Christian heresy with roots in speculative thought, if not a "Hellenization", so much that some modern scholars have delineated two principal expressions of Gnosticism[45]: Valentinianism, which was more "Christian" and hence of special concern to the Church fathers, and Sethianism[46].

Other two big heresies had to hit the Church at the end of the II centuries and with long aftermath until the IV century: Marcionism and Montanism.

Born in Sinope, in Asia Minor, where he was a wealthy Christian ship owner, Marcion came to Rome about A.D.139 and joined the Roman congregation, where he began teaching his own understanding of the Gospel, which was based on an interpretation of the letters of Paul. His views created enough scandal and opposition to bring about his excommunication in A.D. 144. Marcion, therefore, gathered his followers into a separated church, for whom he provided an official canon of sacred books: ten *Letters of Paul* (he did not know of, or decided not to include the *Pastoral Epistles* of Paul) and a form of the

---

44) *Acts*, VIII
45) In example B.A. Pearson, *Ancient Gnosticism: traditions and literature*, Fortress Press 2007
46) K.Rudolph, *Gnosis: The Nature and History of Gnosticism*, HarperOne 1987, passim

Gospel of Luke. The community which he built spread quickly over wide areas and existed as a rival to orthodox churches well into the fifth century. It became especially strong in Syria. Based on his reading of Paul, he learned that the Christian dispensation of a loving and gracious God was founded on the revelation in Christ and inferred that between this Gospel of a loving God and the law-religion of Judaism there was opposition and inconsistency. Rather than reading Jewish scripture as a foreshadowing of Christ, he read them literally and concluded that the God of Moses and the God of Jesus were completely different entities. The latter was a God of love and mercy, the former a God of harsh justice, arbitrary, inconsistent, even tyrannical. This contrast he set forth systematically in his only written work, the *Antitheses*, of which only fragments remain.

Even more dangerous was the so-called "movement of the New Prophecy", better known as Montanism after its founder Montanus, a convert to Christianity. Around A.D. 170 he began to proclaim to his fellow believers that he was a prophet, that he was the very mouthpiece of that Spirit which the Lord had promised would *"teach all things and guide into all truth"*[47]. Montanus was soon joined by two women, Priscilla and Maximilla, who like him delivered oracles in a state of ecstasy, speaking not in their own persons but in that of the Holy Spirit. Montanus and his companions represented a revival of the apocalyptic spirit and announced the forthcoming end of the world: the Lord was about to return, and the new Jerusalem would be set up in the vicinity of the town of Pepuza in Phrygia. As preparation for the end of all things they purified themselves and cut themselves loose from their attachments to society. The "Phrygians", as they were frequently called, fasted longer and more elaborately than other Christians and

---

47) John 14:26; 16:13

discouraged marriage. The movement spread with great rapidity and was known in Rome and the West by the end of a decade. Montanism made its most famous convert in the North African Christian writer Tertullian who was attracted by its seriousness and moral rigor. The bishops of Asia Minor eventually held synods to deal with the "Phrygian problem" and in the end condemned the "New Prophecy" but it remained influential in some regions for quite some time, and was still in existence in North Africa when Augustine came on the scene[48].
Emerging from the theological conflicts with Gnosticism and Montanism was a normative "early Catholicism" which represented a fresh development of Christian tradition. One sign and form of this development was the increased prominence and authority given to creedal or confessional formulas. Up to this time, of course, such formulas had played a role in the Church and had been taken from the teaching of Paul[49] or the writings of Justin Martyr[50]. Most central was the confession of faith which constituted the formula of baptism. By the middle of the II century, the "baptismal confession" was triadic in shape: candidates were asked three questions, to each of which they replied "I believe", and with each of these affirmations and the washings which accompanied them, the candidates were understood to be baptized *"in the name of the Father and of the Son and of the Holy Spirit"*. It is not, therefore, strange that in II century debates about the meaning of the Christian belief appeal was made to the baptismal confession as embodying necessary commitments in formulation. This appeal took the form of insistence upon a "rule" (in Greek: "kanon"), that was variously called the "rule of truth", "rule of faith", "ecclesiastical rule", "tradition" or "kerygma". The "rule" was

---

48) In relation to Marcionism and Montanism: E.Ferguson, *Cit.*, p.107-129
49) 1 Cor .15:3ff
50) In particular from Justin Martyr, *1 Apol.*, XXXXII.4

essentially the syllabus of the instruction through which new believers learned the meaning of the baptismal faith of the Church and, not surprisingly, it often followed the triadic formulation of the baptismal confession[51].

Alongside the "Kanon" or rule provided by traditional confessional formulas, the II century Church, through its debates with Gnosticism and Marcionites established the core of another rule: namely the "canon" of New Testament Scriptures. The procedure by which the formulation of this collection came about was informal and decentralized, a drawn out affair of increasing consensus which was completed more or less in the fourth century. This development involved three simultaneous processes. The first was a growing recognition of the need for a fixed written tradition, especially where the teachings of Jesus were concerned. The second was a process by which such Christian writings as the *Gospels* and the *Apostolic Letters* were acknowledged to have the same essential place in the life of the churches as the Jewish Scriptures and so came to be cited and treated in the same way. The third was the complex business of deciding which Christian writings qualified for this status. On this last issue, two criteria were employed. Books were established as "canonical" if they were regularly read at the liturgical assemblies of the churches, and if they were thought to be apostolic, that is, if they could reasonably be regarded as written by an apostle or by some other person of the founding generation whose testimony was identical with that of the apostles. These two criteria did not always agree, and there were debates about such writings as the *Epistle to the Hebrews* (which the Roman church rightly suspected of not being an authentic Pauline letter) or *Hermas' Shepherd*, which, while clearly not apostolic, was established in liturgical use. A third more informal criterion was that of doctrine. The *Gospel of John*, in

---

51) W. Walker, *Cit.*, p.114-119

example, was for a long time suspect because of the interest Gnostics and followers of the New Prophecy had taken in it. Its establishment as canonical was no doubt owed both to its widespread use and to the fact that an apostolic name was associated with it. By the time of Justin Martyr at least the synoptic Gospels (Matthew, Mark, and Luke) were in liturgical use at Rome, and by the turn of the III century the basic canon of the New testament was firmly established[52].

With the establishing of the basic tool of preaching, also the structure of the Church became more and more formalized. Throughout the II and III centuries, the word "church" continued to denote primarily the assembly of Christians in a particular place or "polis". Whatever the size and complexity of the congregation, its unity was represented in the fact that the local bishop was the leader and pastor of the entire congregation. Chosen by the congregation, the bishop was ordained with laying-on of hands by neighboring bishops, an indication of the fact that in this pastoral charge he was the representative not only of the community to which he belonged but also of the universal Church. Once elected and ordained, he was the ruler in the congregation, administered the communitarian financial affairs, was the principal teacher of the congregation, chose and ordained its other ministers (presbyters, deacons, and others), enforced their discipline and presided at its baptismal and eucharistic assemblies. The III century saw a growth in the number of offices or orders that served the churches. Increasingly distinguished from the laity, the occupants of these offices and orders included not only bishop, deacons and presbyters, but also, from time to time, lectors, widows, sub-deacons, virgins, deaconesses, catechists, acolytes, exorcists, and doorkeepers. Most prominent among these officeholders were undoubtedly the deacons, who, as the

---

52) *Ibidem*, pp. 129-146

bishop's personal assistants, did not only play an important liturgical role but also were in the direct charge of carrying out the charitable work of the community[53]. With this progressive formalization of duties and offices, the whole Church body became more and more important also in the eyes of the empire, which acted towards it in the same form it had acted along the centuries towards any center of power appealing on the people: alternatively taking no interest in it or attacking it.

In some occasion the role of the imperial persecutions in Christian life has been a little overstated: actually it is very possible that, as held by some historians already at the beginning of the XX century[54], the average Christian was not much affected by the persecutions and just Christian "extremists", priests and leaders, really attracted the attention of angry pagans. Everybody[55] knows about Nero's persecution, which, although being rather hard and cruel, was much more a sort of personal more than political or social persecution, meant to find a possible scapegoat for the emperor's harsh actions more than to stop the influence of a Church which, although in growth, was not still particularly significant in the imperial variegated religious world. The persecution, for sure a cruel one, ended anyway in A.D. 68 and for some time Christians were quite ignored by the power with only a few recrudescences from time to time. So, under Domitian (A.D. 81-96), an edict forbade the Jewish and Christian worships, considered subversive for

---

53) T.Dowley, *Cit.*, pp.72-75
54) In example: H. B. Workman, *Persecution in the Early Church*, Oxford University Press, 1906-1980, passim
55) About the history of pre-Diocletian persecutions: L.H. Canfield, *The Early Persecutions Of The Christians (Studies in History, Economics, and Public Law)*, Lawbook Exchange, 2005, passim and G.de Ste.Croix, M.Whitby, J.Streeter, *Christian Persecution, Martyrdom, and Orthodoxy*, Oxford University Press, 2006, passim

their denial to sacrifice to the emperor, but many historians[56] even deny the existence of a persecution; under Trajan (A.D. 112-117), as stated also by Pliny the Younger[57], the Christians were considered by the emperor "dangerous" but the provincial governors were always suggested to keep a "light hand" in investigating about them; under Marcus Aurelius (A.D. 161-180), the personal aversion of the stoic emperor towards the Christian idea of an afterlife didn't result in particular cruelties but mainly in administrative sanctions and the only bloody episode was the already mentioned popular uprising in Lyon of A.D. 77. Quite curiously, the following persecutions were mainly due to popular requests: the emperor Septimus Severus (A.D. 193- 211), in example, may not have been personally ill-disposed towards Christians, but the Church was gaining power and making many converts and this led to popular anti-Christian feeling and persecution in Carthage, Alexandria, Rome and Corinth between about A.D. 202 and A.D. 210, leading the emperor to enact a law prohibiting the spread of Christianity and Judaism and taking to the death of possibly more than 150 martyrs.

It is rather strange to note that, but for Nero's one, the real hard persecutions started only in the III century, 200 years after the beginning of the Church. The first documentable empire-wide persecution took place under Maximinus Thrax (A.D. 235-238), though only the clergy were sought out. Christian sources[58] aver that a decree was issued requiring public sacrifice, a formality equivalent to a testimonial of allegiance to the emperor and the established order. Decius (A.D. 250-251) authorized roving commissions visiting the cities and villages to supervise the

---

56) From E.T.Merrill, *Essays in Early Christian History*, Macmillan, 1924, passim to L.L.Thompson, *The Book of Revelation: Apocalypse and Empire*, Oxford University Press 1990, passim

57) Pliny the Younger, *Epistulae*, X.96

58) Notably Thascius Caecilius Cyprianus, *De Laude Martyrii*, III

execution of the sacrifices and to deliver written certificates to all citizens who performed them. Christians were often given opportunities to avoid further punishment by publicly offering sacrifices or burning incense to Roman gods, and were accused by the Romans of impiety when they refused. Refusal was punished by arrest, imprisonment, torture, and executions. Christians fled to safe havens in the countryside and some purchased their certificates, called "libelli". Several councils held at Carthage debated the extent to which the community should accept these lapsed Christians. The decree of Maximinus remained effective also under Valerianus (A.D. 257-59) and, since A.D. 258, it got hardened (passing, in case of denial to sacrifice to the emperor, from the requisition of properties to the exile in A.D. 257, to death punishment in A.D. 258). When, anyway, in A.D. 260, the emperor Valerian, campaigning against the Persians, was defeated and captured by Sapor, his son, colleague and successor, Gallienus (A.D. 253-268), thereupon revoked his father's edict of persecution, and for the next 44 years the Christian churches enjoyed a period of respite from official persecution. By the end of this period, Christianity was represented in all parts of the empire and its adherents may have numbered as many as five millions, a significant if not large minority of the population. Until that moment, the losses among the Christians for the persecutions, although considerable, had been quite limited. Historians don't agree on the exact number of death, going from an estimated 1500[59] to an estimated 15.000[60] (anyway less than in last 50 years), but times were changing and also persecutions were destined to become harder. In the III century, paganism itself experienced a shift in religious mood. Attention was less focused on the many

---

59) K.Curtis, C.P. Thiede, *From Christ to Constantine: The Trial and Testimony of the Early Church*, Christian History Institute, 1992, p.14
60) E.Gibbon, *Cit.*, p. 302

gods of the classic religion, but gave more attention to the transcendently holy and life giving God whose power the lesser gods represented. This development is manifest particularly on the imperial cult. Emperors, human beings as they were, were no longer seen as gods. Rather they were seen as persons who, in virtue of their office, were "begotten of the gods", sharing in their mortal way the holiness of the Divine and enjoying its protection. Behind this shift in the sense of the imperial cult lay the III century development of solar monotheism, worship of the life-giving sun as a symbol of the ultimate God who is the source of all things[61]. The emperor Aurelian built a great temple to the Unconquered Sun, which he intended to be the center of the religious life of the empire. Christians in the IV century could find no better way of rivaling this popular deity than by using his birthday, December 25th (the winter solstice), to celebrate the birth of Christ, the Sun of Righteousness.

Here we come to the clue point and, getting chronologically closer to year of the council, we reach the core of the elements useful to a deeper understanding of the following events.

After what we have seen about the empire of Diocletian, we can say that his goals in getting the throne were actually three: to stop the disruption of the empire, to re-establish an imperial control on all provinces and to build a new dignity for the imperial role. To understand the reasons of his cruel persecutions against the Christians we must start from this point, asking to ourselves: "how could the Christians be an obstacle towards the achievement of one of this goals?"

Actually, in fact, the beginning of the persecutions is at least mysterious: Diocletian becomes emperor in A.D. 284 and up to A.D. 299 Christians live under his kingdom in absolute peace: they are allowed to build a church near the imperial palace,

---

61) R.Beck, *The Religion of the Mithras Cult in the Roman Empire: Mysteries of the Unconquered Sun*, Oxford University Press, 2007, pp. 11-17

many Christian provincial governors are appointed and even Diocletian's wife, Prisca, and daughter, Valeria, became Christians[62]. Eusebius, a contemporary of Diocletian, underlines *"the glory and the liberty with which the doctrine of piety was honored"*[63] and even if, just a few lines below, he points out that the clerics and laity *"fell into laxity and sloth, and envied and reviled each other, and were almost, as it were, taking up arms against one another [...] casting aside the bond of piety [....]"*[64], the idea to be a sort of God's punishment seems to be very far from the intentions of Diocletian. So, what happens in A.D. 299 to change the emperor's mind towards a religion he had quietly accepted in his own family?

T.B. Scannell, at the voice "Diocletian" of the *Catholic Encyclopedia*, still considered, in its often revised on-line edition, the official cultural voice of the Catholic Church, writes: *"Had Diocletian remained sole emperor, he would probably have allowed this toleration to continue undisturbed. It was his subordinate Galerius who first induced him to turn persecutor. These two rulers of the East, at a council held at Nicomedia in 302, resolved to suppress Christianity throughout the empire."*[65] This interpretation, but for being extremely vague, seem also quite imprecise, giving too much importance to the role of Galerius who, although being a quite rough man and surely a convinced pagan, most probably hadn't neither the strength nor the opportunity to try to move the emperor to a persecution against an already strong and large group of potential opponents of the imperial policy in a moment of

---

62) D.S.Potter, *The Roman Empire at Bay: AD 180–395*, Routledge, 2005, pp.202-211
63) Eusebius, *Ecclesiastical History*, VIII.1
64) *Ibidem*
65) Written by T.B. Scannell. Transcribed by W.G. Kofron. *The Catholic Encyclopedia*, Volume V. Published 1909. New York: Robert Appleton Company. Nihil Obstat, May 1, 1909. Remy Lafort, Censor. Imprimatur. +John M. Farley, Archbishop of New York

extremely wobbly stability of the empire, a group, moreover, dangerously nesting even in Diocletian's palace.

Perhaps it's much better to turn to the reasons given to the persecution by the one for a long time considered the historical voice of the persecuted: Lactantius. The Christian rhetor records that, at Antioch some time in A.D. 299, the emperors were engaged in sacrifice and divination in an attempt to predict the future. The haruspices were unable to read the sacrificed animals, and failed to do so after repeated trials. The master haruspex eventually declared that this failure was the result of interruptions in the process caused by profane men: certain Christians in the imperial household were seen to have made the sign of the cross in an attempt to create a defense against the demons called into service in the pagan ceremonies. The emperors, angry at this turn of events, declared that all members of the court need perform their own sacrifice. Following this, they sent letters to the military command, requiring the entire army to either perform the required sacrifices or else face discharge[66].

Although all historians agree on the religious conservatism of Diocletian[67], it seem quite strange that an isolated event could, alone, completely turn the mind of a cute politician like him. The passage is, anyway, very important as it gives fundamental clues to understand the real reasons of the imperial decrees. We have seen that one of the pillars of the political strategy of Diocletian was the building of an image of the emperor as a link with the gods (or God) able to restore the majesty of a role which, with the continuous turmoils of the previous eras had totally lost its halo of sacredness. That halo was also fundamental to re-build trust and devotion in an army which

---

66) Lucius Caecilius Firmianus Lactantius, *Epitome of the Divine Institutions*, X.1-5
67) In example: H.G. Pagetown, *Diocletian*, Harvey 2006, p. 41

had to be, as it had been in the past, the backbone of the reformed imperial body. Most probably Diocletian understood (and perhaps the episode told by Lactantius was just the last drop in this process) that the fast spreading of Christianity was a sort of weak ring in the chain. Not only real Christians would have never consented, inside of their hearts, to worship the emperor and to trust in him, but they, somehow, also despised the idea to trust in anyone but their God. Considering that a big slice of the Roman army was rapidly converting, the diffusion of Christianity could have, therefore, noxious consequences of unbearable range against the success of the imperial plans.

The actions taken by Diocletian are characterized by what we would now call a "policy of progression": as seen before, the first wave of persecution was only directed to the court and to the army and was, practically, a demonstrative act meant to obtain a full submission from those closer to the power and having key roles in his political plans. Anyway, affairs quieted very soon after the initial turmoil. New persecutions started back, but this time against Manicheans, in A.D. 302 when, being the emperor in Alexandria, he approved and supported a campaign of the proconsul of Africa against this sect. Also in this case the reasons moving the emperor seem to be just political. He found much to be offended by in Manichean religion: its novelty, its alien origins, the way it corrupted the morals of the Roman race and its inherent opposition to long-standing religious traditions were all elements in total opposition to the "conservative reform" brought on by his establishment.[68] It looks like the expanding of the persecutions to all the Christians of the empire in the autumn of the same year was, again, due to a single episode provoking a sort of "domino

---

68) T.D. Barnes, *Constantine and Eusebius*, Harvard University Press, 2006, p. 24

effect". According to Lactantius[69], Diocletian was in Antioch in the autumn of A.D. 302. The deacon Romanus had come to the city from Caesarea Maritima, in Syria Palaestina and seeing many in the city visiting the pagan temples, was angered. In protest, he visited a court while preliminary sacrifices were taking place and interrupted the ceremonies, decrying the act in a loud voice. He was arrested and sentenced to be set aflame, but Diocletian overruled the decision, and decided that Romanus should have his tongue removed instead. This being done, Romanus was sent to prison, where he would be executed on November 17th, A.D. 303. The arrogance of this Christian displeased Diocletian, and he left the city and made for Nicomedia for the winter, accompanied by Galerius.

Here it is probable that the younger Caesar cold have played an important role in relation to the following events. At this point, Diocletian was probably sure that the fracture between the Christians and the empire he was setting was irremediable but it is also probable that, fearful of possible riots able to mine the unsure existing balance, he wanted to act in a quite surgical way: again Lactantius[70] informs us that his intent was only to forbid Christians from the bureaucracy and military but that Galerius pushed for a total eradication of the "Christian disease". Why? Lactantius speaks about a vaticination of the oracle of Apollo at Didyma but, although they actually were two good "old religion" believers, both Diocletian and Galerius were mainly politicians, surely basing their decisions on facts more than on the obscure words of an oracle. The point is that these events took place in A.D.303, that's to say in the year in which Diocletian was preparing his succession and Galerius was his designed successor. Galerius, on his hand, had a big problem: he was a good soldier, but, as the following events demonstrated, a

---

69) Lucius Caecilius Firmianus Lactantius, *Cit.*, X.6
70) *Ibidem*, X.6-11

quite bad politician, in this period totally faithful to the directives of Diocletian and, therefore, absolutely fanatic of his imperial plans. His idea was that only a coming back to the traditional cult of the emperor could maintain the empire united. His Western counterpart, Constantius Chlorus, but for being older, was much cuter than him and was well known for his, if not affection, at least goodwill towards the Christians[71]. It is, therefore not impossible that the plan of Galerius was to bet on the support of the pagan majority of the army and of the population, trying to weaken the Christians, in prevision of the possible formation of arrays in the immediately post-Diocletian period. Unfortunately, this last, probably already affected by deep depression, or simply not willing to displease the man he had chosen as his successor, assented to start the progressive massacre that passed to history with the name of "Great Persecution" and that cost the life of more than 3500 martyrs[72]. And actually, even politically, this was for sure a wrong move. It is uncertain exactly how much support there was for policies of persecution within the aristocracy. Surely the emperor Constantius disapproved this policy (and, in fact, he continued to extend toleration to the Christians in his domain, so that the Christians of Gaul and Britain remained relatively unmolested[73]), but this time also the lower classes demonstrated little of the same enthusiastic support they had had for earlier persecutions: the long-established Christian Church had perhaps simply become another accepted part of their lives, no longer as alien as it had once been.

This last is a key element to understand the following events and the position of Constantine.

We have seen that the succession of the first tetrachy was,

---

71) W. Leadbetter, *Cit.*, Routledge, 2008, pp. 97ff
72) K.Curtis, C.P. Thiede, *Cit.*, p.189
73) A. Samuel, *Constatius and Constantine*, Oxford University Press, 2002, p. 91-96

finally, a total disaster. While anarchy was spreading all over, the persecution, although not as bloody as in its beginnings, went on but, in the continuous changes of alliances of the years after A.D.305, the Christians were no more just a "noxious minority": they could become a precious allied. The first one to realize this element was Galerius who, in fact, just before dying (a thing that brought to the legend of a late conversion reported at the end of the previous chapter), tried an act of extreme alliance with the consistent Christian minority (in particular of Asia) issuing the "Edict of Nicomedia" with which, with the words: "*Wherefore, for this our indulgence, they ought to pray to their God for our safety, for that of the republic, and for their own, that the republic may continue uninjured on every side, and that they may be able to live securely in their homes*"[74], he put an end to the persecutions.

Actually it was too late: the Christians were already betting on another horse (or perhaps another horse was betting on them). And a new era for Christianity was approaching: the era of Constantine.

---

74) Lucius Caecilius Firmianus Lactantius, *Cit.*, XXXIV

I.3) CONSTANTINE: HIS TIME, HIS EMPIRE, HIS CHURCH

At the end of the first chapter, we left Constantine about to invade Italy with his troops: with Galerius dead in A.D. 311, the main authority amongst the emperors had been removed, leaving them to struggle for dominance, so that in the East Licinius and Maximinus Daia fought for supremacy and in the West Constantine began a war with Maxentius.

When in A.D. 312 Constantine invades Italy, Maxentius is believed to have had up to four times as many troops, although they were inexperienced and undisciplined.

Since this moment on, the life of the emperor, as reported by the majority of the chronicles of his time (ofter largely used by the following historiography up to recent times), seems something like a sort of mixture between a fairy tale and an hagiography. Let's try to briefly summarize the main elements anyone can find in the majority of history books[75].

Brushing aside the opposition in battles at Augusta Taurinorum (Turin) and Verona, Constantine marched on Rome. Constantine later claimed to have had a vision on the way to Rome, during the night before the battle. In this dream he supposedly saw the 'Chi-Ro', the symbol of Christ, shining above the sun. Seeing this as a divine sign, it is said that the emperor had his soldiers paint the symbol on their shields. Following this, Constantine went on to defeat the numerically stronger army of Maxentius at the Battle at the Milvian Bridge (October A.D. 312).

Constantine's opponent Maxentius, together with thousands of

---

75) In example: J. Burckhardt, *The Age of Constantine the Great*, University of California Press, 1983, passim; R.MacMullen, *Christianizing the Roman empire: A. D. 100-400*, Yale University Press, 1986, passim; R.Stark, *The Rise of Christianity: How the Obscure, Marginal, Jesus Movement Became the Dominant Religious Force*, HarperOne, 1997, passim

his soldiers, drowned as the bridge of boats his force was retreating over collapsed.

Constantine saw this victory as directly related to the vision he had had the night before.

Henceforth Constantine saw himself as an 'emperor of the Christian people'. If this made him a Christian is the subject of some debate. But Constantine, who only had himself baptized on his deathbed, is generally understood as the first Christian emperor of the Roman world.

With his victory over Maxentius at the Milvian Bridge, Constantine became the dominant figure in the empire. The senate warmly welcomed him to Rome and the two remaining emperors, Licinius and Maximinus II Daia could do little else but agree to his demand that he henceforth should be the senior Augustus. It was in this senior position that Constantine ordered Maximinus II Daia to cease his repression of the Christians.

Despite this turn toward Christianity, Constantine remained for some years still very tolerant of the old pagan religions. Particularly the worship of the Sol Invictus was still closely related with him for some time to come, as can be seen by the massive use of the symbol of the sun during his whole reign[76].

Then in A.D. 313 Licinius defeated Maximinus II Daia. This left only two emperors.

At first both tried to live peacefully aside each other, Constantine in the West, Licinius in the East. In A.D. 313 they met at Mediolanum (Milan), where Constantine promulgated the famous Edict making Christianity the state religion and where Licinius even married Constantine's sister Constantia and restated that Constantine was the senior Augustus. Yet, it was made clear that Licinius would make his own laws in the East, without the need to consult Constantine. Further, it was agreed

---

76) R.MacMullen, *Cit.*, p. 183

that Licinius would return property to the Christian Church which had been confiscated in the Eastern provinces.

As time went on, Constantine seemed to become ever more involved with the Christian Church. He appeared at first to have very little grasp of the basic beliefs governing Christian faith, but gradually he possibly became more acquainted with them, so much that he even sought to resolve theological disputes among the Church itself[77].

In this role, as we will see, he summoned the bishops of the Western provinces to Arelate (Arles) in A.D. 314, after the so-called Donatist schism had split the church in Africa. If this willingness to resolve matters through peaceful debate showed one side of Constantine, then his brutal enforcement of the decisions reached at such meetings showed the other: evidently Constantine was also capable of persecuting Christians, if they were deemed to be the 'wrong type of Christians'.

In the meanwhile, problems with Licinius arose when Constantine appointed his brother-in-law Bassianus as Caesar for Italy and the Danubian provinces. If the principle of the tetrarchy, established by Diocletian, still in theory defined government, then Constantine as senior Augustus had the right to do this. And yet, Diocletian's principle's would have demanded that he appointed an independent man on merit. But Licinius saw in Bassianus little else than a puppet of Constantine. If the Italian territories were Constantine's, then the important Danubian military provinces were under the control of Licinius. If Bassianus was indeed Constantine's puppet it would have meant a serious gain of power by Constantine. And so, to prevent his opponent from yet further increasing his power, Licinius managed to persuade Bassianus to revolt against Constantine in A.D. 314 or A.D. 315.

The rebellion was easily put down, but the involvement of

---

77) *Ibidem*, p. 191

Licinius was discovered too. And this discovery made war inevitable. But considering the situation responsibility for the war, must lie with Constantine. It appears that he was simply unwilling to share power and hence sought to find means by which to bring about a fight.

For a while neither side acted and, instead, both camps preferred to prepare for the contest ahead. Then, in A.D. 316, Constantine attacked with his forces. In July or August at Cibalae in Pannonia he defeated Licinius larger army, forcing his opponent to retreat.

The next step was taken by Licinius, when he announced Aurelius Valerius Valens to be the new emperor of the West. It was an attempt to undermine Constantine, but it clearly failed to work. Soon after, another battle followed, at Campus Ardiensis in Thrace. This time, however, neither side gained victory, as the battle proved indecisive.

Once more, the two sides reached a treaty (March 1st, A.D. 317). Licinius surrendered all Danubian and Balkan provinces, with the exception of Thrace, to Constantine. In effect this was little else but a confirmation of the actual balance of power, as Constantine had indeed conquered these territories and controlled them. Despite his weaker position, Licinius, though, still retained complete sovereignty over his remaining Eastern dominions. Also as part of the treaty, Licinius' alternative Western Augustus was put to death.

The final part of this agreement reached at Serdica was the creation of three new Caesars. Crispus and Constantine II were both sons of Constantine, and Licinius the Younger was the infant son of the Eastern emperor and his wife Constantia.

For a short while the empire should enjoy peace. But soon the situation began to deteriorate again. If Constantine acted more and more in favor of the Christians, then Licinius began to disagree. From A.D. 320 onwards, Licinius began to suppress the Christian church in his Eastern provinces and also began ejecting any Christians from government posts.

Another problem arose regarding the consulships. These were by now widely understood as positions in which emperors would groom their sons as future rulers. Their treaty at Serdica had hence proposed that appointments should be made by mutual agreement. Licinius though believed Constantine favored his own sons when granting these positions[78].

And so, in clear defiance of their agreements, Licinius appointed himself and his two sons consuls for the Eastern provinces for the year A.D. 322.

With this declaration it was clear that hostilities between the two sides would soon begin afresh. Both sides began to prepare for the struggle ahead.

In A.D. 323 Constantine created yet another Caesar by elevating his third son Constantius II to this rank.

If the Eastern and Western halves of the empire were hostile towards one another, then in A.D. 323 a reason was soon found to start a new civil war. Constantine, while campaigning against Gothic invaders, strayed into Licinius' Thracian territory.

It is well possible he did so on purposely in order to provoke a war. Be that as it may, Licinius took this as the reason to declare war in spring A.D. 324.

But it was once again Constantine who moved to attack first with 120000 infantry and 10000 cavalry against Licinius' 150000 infantry and 15000 cavalry based at Hadrianopolis. On July 3rd A.D. 324 he severely defeated Licinius' forces at Hadrianopolis and shortly after his fleet won victories at sea.

Licinius fled across the Bosporus to Asia Minor (Turkey), but Constantine, having brought with him a fleet of two thousand transport vessels, ferried his army across the water and forced the decisive battle of Chrysopolis, where he utterly defeated Licinius (September 18th, A.D. 324).

---

78) J. Burckhardt, *Cit*, pp. 207ff

Licinius was imprisoned and later executed.
Alas Constantine was sole emperor of the entire Roman world.
Soon after his victory in A.D. 324, he outlawed pagan sacrifices, now feeling far more at liberty to enforce his new religious policy. The treasures of pagan temples were confiscated and used to pay for the construction of new Christian churches. Gladiatorial contests were outruled and harsh new laws were issued prohibiting sexual immorality. Jews in particular were forbidden from owning Christian slaves.
Constantine continued the reorganization of the army, begun by Diocletian, re-affirming the difference between frontier garrisons and mobile forces, the mobile forces consisting largely of heavy cavalry which could quickly move to trouble spots. The presence of Germans continued to increase during his reign.
The praetorian guard which had held such influence over the empire for so long, was finally disbanded. Their place was taken by the mounted guard, largely consisting of Germans, which had been introduced under Diocletian.
As a law maker Constantine was terribly severe.
Edicts were passed by which the sons were forced to take up the professions of their fathers. Not only was this terribly harsh on such sons who sought a different career, but by making the recruitment of veteran's sons compulsory, and enforcing it ruthlessly with harsh penalties, widespread fear and hatred was caused.
Also his taxation reforms created extreme hardship. City dwellers were obliged to pay a tax in gold or silver, the "chrysargyron". This tax was levied every four years, beating and torture being the consequences for those to poor to pay. Parents are said to have sold their daughters into prostitution in order to pay the "chrysargyron"[79].

---

79) J. Burckhardt, *Cit.*, pp. 213-214

Under Constantine, any girl who ran away with her lover was burned alive, any man who should assist in such a matter had molten lead poured into her mouth, rapists were burned at the stake and also their women victims were punished, if they had been raped away from home, as they, according to Constantine, should have no business outside the safety of their own homes[80].

But Constantine is perhaps most famous for the great city which came to bear his name - Constantinople.

He came to the conclusion that Rome had ceased to be a practical capital for the empire from which the emperor could exact effective control over its frontiers.

For a while he set up court in different places; Treviri (Trier), Arelate (Arles), Mediolanum (Milan), Ticinum, Sirmium and Serdica (Sofia).

Then, he decided on the ancient Greek city of Byzantium and, on November 8th, A.D. 324, Constantine created his new capital there, renaming it Constantinopolis (City of Constantine).

He was careful to maintain Rome's ancient privileges, and the new senate founded in Constantinople was of a lower rank, but he clearly intended it to be the new center of the Roman world. Measures to encourage its growth were introduced, most importantly the diversion of the Egyptian grain supplies, which had traditionally gone to Rome, to Constantinople, for a Roman-style corn-dole was introduced, granting every citizen a guaranteed ration of grain[81].

In A.D. 325 Constantine held the council of Nicea and, as we will see, it gave him the final title of patron of the Christian Church although a few months later, in A.D. 326, on suspicion of adultery or treason, he had his own eldest son Crispus

---

80) *Ibidem*, p. 216
81) T.Julian, *Constantine, Christianity and Constantinople*, Trafford Publishing 2006, pp.76-78

executed.

One account of the events tells of Constantine's wife Fausta falling in love with Crispus, who was her stepson, and made an accusation of him committing adultery only once she had been rejected by him, or because she simply wanted Crispus out of the way, in order to let her sons arrive to the throne unhindered. Then again, Constantine had only a month before passed a strict law against adultery and might have felt obliged to act. And so Crispus was executed at Pola in Istria, although after this execution Constantine's mother Helena convinced the emperor of Crispus' innocence and that Fausta's accusation had been false. Escaping the vengeance of her husband, Fausta killed herself at Treviri[82].

A brilliant general, Constantine was a man of boundless energy and determination.

Had Constantine defeated all contenders to the Roman throne, the need to defend the borders against the Northern barbarians still remained.

In the autumn of A.D. 328, accompanied by Constantine II, he campaigned against the Alemanni on the Rhine. This was followed in late A.D. 332 by a large campaign against the Goths along the Danube until, in A.D. 336, he had re-conquered much of Dacia, once annexed by Trajan and abandoned by Aurelian.

In A.D. 333 Constantine's fourth son Constans was raised to the rank of Caesar, with the clear intent to groom him, alongside his brothers, to jointly inherit the empire. Also Constantine's nephews Flavius Dalmatius (who may have been raised to Caesar by Constantine in A.D. 335) and Hannibalianus were raised as future emperors. Evidently they also were intended to be granted their shares of power at Constantine's death.

How, after his own experience of the tetrarchy, Constantine saw

---

82) J. Burckhardt, *Cit.*, pp. 238-246

it possible that all five of these heirs should rule peaceably alongside each other, is hard to understand.

In old age now, Constantine planned a last great campaign, which was intended to conquer Persia. He is said to be intended to receive the baptism as a Christian on the way to the frontier, in the waters of the river Jordan, just as Jesus had been baptized there by John the Baptist.

As the ruler of these soon to be conquered territories, Constantine even placed his nephew Hannibalianus on the throne of Armenia, with the title of King of Kings, which had been the traditional title borne by the kings of Persia.

But this scheme was not to come to anything, for in the spring of A.D. 337, Constantine fell ill. Realizing that he was about to die, he asked to be baptized. This was performed on his deathbed by Eusebius, bishop of Nicomedia[83].

Constantine died on May 22nd, A.D. 337 at the imperial villa at Ankyrona and his body was carried to the church of the Holy Apostles, his mausoleum. Had his own wish to be buried in Constantinople caused outrage in Rome, the Roman senate still decided on his deification: a strange decision as it elevated him, the supposed first Christian emperor, to the status of an old pagan deity.

So far, the more or less official biography of Constantine as it emerges from the majority of the sources: surely the one of a man with lights and shadows but also the one of a great emperor. Unfortunately also a quite imprecise one, in particular in respect to the most important element in the context of our research: his relation towards the Church and Christianity.

The main reason of this lack of precision is that, although the ancient sources for Constantine's reign are, as mentioned, relatively many and normally quite detailed, they have been generally strongly influenced by the official propaganda of the

---

83) R.Stark, *Cit.*, p. 171

period and are one-sided in judgment[84].

Actually there are no surviving complete histories or biographies dealing with Constantine's life and rule but the nearest replacement is Eusebius of Caesarea's *Vita Constantini*, a work that is a mixture of eulogy and hagiography[85]: written between A.D. 335 and ca. A.D. 339, the the work focuses on the religious and moral character of Constantine's life[86] and extols the emperor's moral virtues and religious faith[87]. Also Lactantius' *De Mortibus Persecutorum*, we already met, a polemical Christian pamphlet on the reigns of Diocletian and the tetrarchy, provides valuable but tendentious detail on Constantine's early life, always set in opposition to his "evil" predecessors[88]. Finally, the ecclesiastical histories of Socrates, Sozomen, and Theodoret describe the ecclesiastic disputes of Constantine's later reign[89]: written during the reign of Theodosius II (A.D. 408–50), a century after Constantine's reign, these ecclesiastic historians obscure the events and theologies of the Constantine period through misdirection,

---

84) B.Bleckmann, *Sources for the History of Constantine*, in AA.VV., *The Cambridge Companion to the Age of Constantine*, Cambridge University Press, 2005, pp.14-31

85) H. A. Drake, *What Eusebius Knew: The Genesis of the "Vita Constantini"*, in *Classical Philology*, Vol. 83, No. 1, The University of Chicago Press 1988, pp. 20-38

86) T.D. Barnes, *Constantine and Eusebius*, Harvard University Press, 1984, pp.273ff;

87) An aim stated in the work's opening passages. In the *Vita*, Eusebius creates an image of a pious, kind, and noble Constantine but the positiveness of this image, however, has been so tendentious that the work has sometimes been called a "tissue of lies" (in example by N. Lenski in AA.VV., *The Cambridge Companion to the Age of Constantine, Cit.*, p.8)

88) C.S. Mackay, *Lactantius and the Succession to Diocletian*, in Classical Philology, Vol. 94, No. 2, The University of Chicago Press, 1999, p. 205

89) Each is principally based on the lost histories of Gelasius of Caesarea, and each continues the work of Eusebius' ecclesiastic history. Barnes, *Cit.*, p.225

misrepresentation and deliberate obscurity[90].

So, let's try to analyze the most important moments of Constantine's religious life through the lens of the historical science.

Having to state which are the fundamental points creating the image of Constantine as a "saint" before the council we can list them in:
- the vision before the battle of the Milvian Bridge in A.D. 312 and the choice of the Chi-Ro as legionary symbol;
- the Edict of Milan of A.D. 313, freeing the Christians to worship their God;
- the anti-Donatist persecution in A.D.314;
- the pro-Christians laws after A.D.318 and the anti-pagans laws after A.D.324.

Actually, each one of these clue moments can be seen under a different light than the one of a Christian emperor chosen by Eusebius, Lactantius and all the other writers.

Let's start with the possibly most famous episode of Constantine's life, the vision of the "IN HOC SIGNO VINCES"[91].

It's almost a pity to destroy such a wonderful story, but, unluckily too many elements don't match.

Let's imagine the situation: Constantine has the privilege a vision directly from God, who makes him win the most important battle of his life. What would anyone have done if not converting immediately to this clearly unique and powerful God? But so, how to explain the fact that the enormous arch

---

90) *Ibidem*, p.226
91) Eusebius, *Vita Constantini* 1.28. "Hoc Signo Victor Eris" in Constantine's original Latin, becoming "touto nika" (τούτω νίκα) in Eusebius' Greek. When Eusebius' *Vita* was translated into Latin at the end of the IV century, the original phrasing had been forgotten, and the phrase was translated into variants like "In Hoc Vince", or "In Hoc Signo Vinces" (C.M. Odahl, *Constantine and the Christian empire*, Routledge, 2004, p.184)

that commemorates the battle, built in A.D. 315, still bears the Unconquered Son in three places in reliefs[92]? Why does this emperor, so blessed by God, emanates three coinages (A.D. 317, A.D. 321, A.D. 323) with the figure of the Unconquered Son[93]? Why, still in A.D. 321, instituting a weekly festivity day he writes: *"On the venerable day of the Sun let the magistrates and people residing in cities rest, and let all workshops be closed. In the country however persons engaged in agriculture may freely and lawfully continue their pursuits because it often happens that another day is not suitable for grain-sowing or vine planting; lest by neglecting the proper moment for such operations the bounty of heaven should be lost."*[94]?

This really (even not involving theological problems such as why would Jesus promote the breaking of the second Commandment by giving Constantine a symbol to conquer by and use as a safeguard?[95]) doesn't make sense.

The point is, very probably, that, as Chadwick says, *"Constantine, like his father, worshiped the Unconquered Sun"*[96] and he did it all life long, simply applying a sort of personal syncretism that mixed the figure of Jesus Christ with the one of the divinity in whose cult he had been grown up and which, it's important to remember, was the only official cult accepted in the Roman army since the reign of Aurelian[97]: the Unconquered Sun.

So, what about the symbol on the shields and the vision?

In relation to the symbol on the shields, with all probabilities it was not, as stated only by Christian writers (the mentioned

---

92) V. Armetrano, *L'Arco di Costantino*, Aureliana, 1991, pp.56-61
93) P.M.Bruun, *The Roman Imperial Coinage*, Volume VII, Spink, 2003. pp.83-91
94) *CJ*3.12.2
95) Exodus 20:4
96) H.Chadwick, *The Early Church*, Penguin, 1993, p.127
97) A.S.Hoey, *Official Policy towards Oriental Cults in the Roman Army*, Transactions and Proceedings of the American Philological Association, N.70, 1939, pp. 456-481

Eusebius and Lactantius, then reported by all the others), the Chi-Ro (or "Crismon")

but, once again, the easiest and most common form of representation of the cult of the Unconquered Sun[98]:

In relation to the vision, some think Constantine actually had one and have argued for a meteorological explanation, explaining it as either a "solar halo"[99] or the tail of a meteor[100], but most historians have disputed either the details of the events or their very existence, arguing for a later conversion date (or directly a total lack of conversion) and, thereby, avoiding the historiographic problems of miracles altogether[101]. In reality, the visions were part of Christians' common eschatological expectations in the period: beginning with the *Gospel of Matthew* and continuing on through the *Didache*, the *Apocalypse of Peter*,

---

98) M. Holbourn, *Constantine the Great*, Oxford University Press, 1995, pp. 181ff.

99) O.Nicholson, *Constantine's Vision of the Cross*, in "Vigiliae Christianae" LIV.3, 2000, pp. 309-323

100) D.Whitehouse, *Space impact "saved Christianity"*, BBC News, 23rd June 2003

101) In example: N. Lenski, *Cit.*, p. 71

the *Apocalypse of Elijah*, the appearance of the "Sign of the Son of Man" in the heavens was a common motif preceding the Second Coming of Christ in Christian writings on the "End Times"[102] and Lactantius, knowing this trend in eschatology[103], could have easily inserted it in his account to bear out his statements.

As seen, the clues to think Constantine was (and remained) a pagan exist. It is anyway unquestionable that his policy after A.D. 312 tended to favor the Christians, even if less than what is normally thought.

In example, the Edict of Milan, in A.D. 313, was not exactly, as someone[104], in the line of Lactantius[105] and Eusebius[106], think, a sort of institution of Christianity as state religion in the empire[107], but simply a statement of an already existing situation and a way to confirm decisions already taken in advance: the text usually called the Edict of Milan is, in fact, a letter to the Governor of Bithynia of June A.D. 313, just one of a series of letters issued by Licinius in the territory he conquered from Maximinus in A.D.313. Both toleration of Christian worship and restitution of Christians' properties had already been granted by Constantine in Gaul, Spain and Britain (already in A.D. 306), and by Maxentius in Italy and Africa (in A.D. 306 toleration and in A.D. 310 restitution). Galerius and Licinius had enacted toleration in the Balkans in A.D.311, and Licinius probably extended restitution there in early A.D. 313. Thus the letters which Licinius issued in the names of himself and

---

102) O.Nicholson, *Cit.*, p.313
103) *Ibidem*, p.316
104) In example J.Prescott, *Christianity and Romanity: How Christians Conquered Rome*, Geminal 1992, pp.18-22
105) Lactantius, *Cit.*, XXXIV-XXXV
106) Eusebius, *Historia Ecclesiastica*, VIII-IX
107) Which will take place only in A.D.380 with the Edict of Thessalonki by Theodosius I

Constantine (as was routine for imperial documents, which were formally issued in the names of all legitimate co-rulers) were designed solely to enact toleration and restitution in Anatolia and Oriens, which had been under the rule of Maximinus[108].

Moreover, the Edict, in the form of a joint letter to be circulated among the governors of the East, simply declared that the empire would be neutral with regard to any religious worship, officially removing all obstacles to the practice of Christianity but also of all other religions[109].

So, it's true that the Edict *"was a decisive step from hostile neutrality to friendly neutrality and protection, and prepared the way for the legal recognition of Christianity, as the religion of the empire"*[110] and that it transformed the status of Christianity, as it initiated the period known by Christian historians as the "Peace of the Church" but it is also true that, in itself, it was not so fundamental as believed and, mainly, it was much more and act by Licinius than an act by Constantine.

Also the anti-Donatist "crusade" of A.D. 314 was, finally, nothing more than a sort of administrative act to impose the imperial authority on a determined slice of population and not an act of faith or a particular attitude of Constantine. To understand this point it's enough to have a look to the development of the events.

Donatism began in A.D. 311 when Caecilian became bishop of Carthage. By A.D. 311 a bishop needed ordination by three other bishops. Donatus, a Carthaginian deacon, protested Caecilian's ordination because one of these bishops was a known "traditor". A "traditor" was a clergyman who had obtained a "libellus" or handed over Scripture during the

---

108) J. Curran, *Constantine and the Ancient Cults of Rome: The Legal Evidence*, "Greece & Rome" 2nd Series 43.1, 1996, pp 68-80

109) *Ibidem*

110) P.Schaff, *Nicene and Post-Nicene Fathers*, Vol.2, Hendrickson Publishers, 1990, p.554

persecution and Donatus argued that failure to remain faithful invalidated ordination. When Donatus and his party failed to remove Caecilian, they elected Majorinus as "true Bishop" in A.D. 312. Majorinus died in A.D. 313 and Donatus became the splinter group's bishop. Actually there were also other contributing factors to the Donatist controversy: nationalism, economic unrest, appeals to rigorism and zeal for orthodoxy aided the movement[111] and, somehow, even a certain level of local resistance to a Christian centralized power worked in this sense[112].

Constantine was introduced to the problem when he sent relief money to North Africa: he directed relief funds to the bishops for distribution thinking they would distribute the funds to meet the greatest needs. But the problem was about which Carthaginian bishop should receive the funds. Both bishops claimed orthodoxy and both refused to recognize the other. In addition, since needy Donatist congregations existed outside Carthage they claimed they did not receive their share of relief funds.

Therefore, the emperor appointed Melchiades, the Roman bishop, to investigate. Melchiades and five Gallic bishops summoned Caecilian and ten bishops from each side to Rome. A hasty decision favoring Caecilian followed. The Donatists complained they did not receive a fair hearing. Constantine ordered a second hearing to convene in Arles in 314. Again numerous bishops representing both sides came from throughout the empire although most came from Gaul and Italy. The hearing again exonerated Caecilian although they decided proven "traditors" should be removed from the ministry. The Donatists found this unsatisfying and they

---

111) C.S. Meyer, *Moving Frontiers*, Concordia Publishing House, 1986, p.14
112) D.F. Wright, J.D. Woodbridge, *Public Faith: From Constantine to the Medieval World, A.D. 312-600*, Baker Books, 2005, pp.58ff

appealed directly to Constantine. In a judgment issued in 316 the Emperor said: *"At the investigation I clearly perceived that Caecilian was completely blameless; a man who observed the customary duties of his religion[113], and devoted himself to it as was incumbent upon him. It was plain that no fault could be found in him, such as had been, by the invention of his enemies, alleged against him in his absence"*[114].

It is very possible that the decision of the emperor was due mainly to the reading of the reports from the Italian and Gaul bishops, clearly writing in an anti-Donatist position, or to the excessive severity of the Donatists, which, anyway maintained a memory of the period of hard relations between Christianity and empire, but the element which made the situation come to a head was that the recalcitrant Donatists refused to accept the authority of either the council at Arles or Constantine[115].

Losing patience and, mainly, forecasting the possibility of a break in that unspoken alliance which was being created between Christians and himself since already before the Edict of Milan, Constantine threatened to take care of things. Augustine reports he expressed his ideas to his advisers in this form: *"I am going to make plain to them what kind of worship is to be offered to God... What higher duty have I as emperor than to destroy error and repress rash indiscretions, and so cause all to offer to Almighty God true religion, honest concord and true worship"*[116]. It is clear that with this statement Constantine was expressing at least three different things: the will to stop a noxious dispute, the bases of "Caesaropapism", the formal enacting of a new Christianity-empire alliance.

---

113) It's to note Constantine uses the form "his" and not "our" religion, but this could be just a matter of style or of impartiality

114) Augustine of Hippo, *Augustine: Political Writings*, Cambridge University Press, 2000, pp. 175ff

115) S.Lieu, *Constantine: History, Historiography and Legend*, Routledge, 1998, p.163

116) Augustine of Hippo, *Cit.*, p. 179

At first the emperor ordered the confiscation of Donatist churches and banished their leaders, then he continued harassing Donatists until numerous Donatist martyrs poured out their blood into North African sands. Ultimately Donatists disappeared into the North African desert and the Donatist bodies become "rural" churches opposing Roman policies, bishops and "citified" ways from a very peripheral and undamaging position and, once again, the fact that the imperial persecution was a matter of power and not of faith became further clearer: as soon as the Donatists stopped being a danger for his authority, Constantine withdrew his oppressive measures and started ignoring them, so that the heresy went on until after A.D. 411[117].

What is important, anyway, is the stronger and stronger political link associating Constantine to the Christians. Christianity was a growing and growing power in the empire: it was no more only numerically important, but it was expanding also in the upper classes (normally taking the place of mystery cults) and, mainly it was having a great appeal among the members of the army[118]. It would have been rather stupid by Constantine, who enjoyed a relatively high level of appeal inside of the various Christian Churches spread through the empire, not to make the most of the situation, creating a sort of political connection which, anyway, didn't necessarily mean, for him, a conversion[119] (also as

---

117) B.H. Cooper, *The Free Church Of Ancient Christendom And Its Subjugation Under Constantine*, Kessinger Publishing, 2006, p.328

118) J. Solomon, *The Growth of Christianity in the Roman empire*, Everton Press, 1994, pp.88-91

119) Actually, not even his final baptism is so sure. The longly circulating story of his baptism at Rome by Pope Sylvester in 326, and of the so-called Donation of Constantine, long treated as an argument and justification for the temporal power of the papacy, is completely unhistorical, as already proved by Lorenzo Valla in the XV century (R. Fubini, *Humanism and Truth: Valla Writes against the Donation of Constantine*, Journal of the History of Ideas, LVII.1, 1996, pp. 79–86) but also the account of Eusebius (Eusebius

he probably thought that, worshiping the Unconquered Sun, as seen, he was already somehow a member of "another form" of Christianity).

The alliance Christians-Constantine had to be so clear that it must have been for this reason that, Licinius, having no chance to break such a strong link, in the very moment of his opposition to his "colleague" (A.D. 320), chose "to bet on the opposite horse", attacking the Christians and supporting the last gleams of paganism.

This choice of arrays brought Constantine even closer to Christianity and explains his track from the pro-Christians laws after A.D. 318 to the anti-pagans laws after A.D. 324, a track leading him to emanate laws such as the abolition of crucifixion, the abolition of infanticide, the discouraging of slavery and the suppression of gladiatorial games (which were not, anyway, completely eliminated) and many others. It's obvious that, choosing the Christians as allies, Constantine helped them in many ways: he selected Christian men as his advisers, provided many benefits for the clergy (the clergymen did not have to pay taxes, they did not have to serve in the military and, very often, they were paid good salaries) and contributed greatly to the building of great church buildings in

---

of Caesarea, *Vita Constatini*, IV.64) about the final conversion, the will to be baptized in the Jordan River and the final baptism in Nicomedia at the age of 65 seem to be quite doubtful (T.Roman, *The Myth of a Christian Emperor: Constantine an His links to Christianity*, Rowan Editions 2002, pp. 143-151). Even believing in the eventuality of a truthful report and embracing the theory that in that period infant baptism, though practiced had not yet become a matter of routine in the west (T.M. Finn, *Early Christian Baptism and the Catechumenate: East and West Syria*,The Liturgical Press/Michael Glazier 1992, pp.131-137), the baptism by the arianizing bishop Eusebius of Nicomedia after all the events of Nicea would demonstrate a radical lack of interest of Constantine in the theological debate he had had a great part in.

Jerusalem, Bethlehem, Constantinople and other places[120], creating a sort of virtuous circle which helped in the conversion of new believers and, on the other hand, strengthened his position as (caesaropapistic) leader of the Christianity.

But Constantine was not a theologian, nor a mystic: he was mainly a politician and, more, a former general famous for his strategies. And, as a formal general, he knew very well that nothing can weaken an army (in this case the army of his allies) as internal divisions.

It's under this focus lens that we must observe the most important of his interventions in the Christian field: the council of Nicea.

---

120) J.S. Morningdale, *The policy of Constantine the Great towards Christians*, Absalom, 2001, passim

II

THE COUNCIL

Dr. Lawrence M.F. Sudbury – **Nicea: what it was, what it was not**

II.1) A DIVIDED CHURCH, A DIVIDED EMPIRE

So Constantine had chosen his position towards the Christians: contrarily to what his predecessors had done before him, he had chosen not to oppose Christianity but to support it and, therefore, to be supported by it. His choice, as we have seen, was due to various reasons. Partly, it is unquestionable that he felt the Christian religion as the closest to his own religion: the Unconquered Sun worship. Much more, this alliance was the result of a cute political calculation: the traditional Roman pagan religion was progressively dying, already substituted by mystery cults which anyway, although quite spread out, were meant to be deserved to a limited circle of followers, in opposition to the Christian worship, being ecumenical, giving hope for the afterlife and, therefore, rapidly spreading among all levels of population, including the army.

Finally, the last (but not least) cause of his support, was that his sovereignty on the empire was not uncontested and needed partisans, so that the choice of such a wide-spread group of supporters meant also a growth of his internal power.

This alliance was, therefore, in his vision, a sort of "do-ut-des" in which he gave much (safety, power, importance, money, finally the possibility of a spectacular cult growth) asking in exchange a simple but very clear think: to have a recognized patronage on the body of the Church and, consequently, to have weight in its governance.

The enormous problem for him was to maintain his allied and supporting church a powerful organism inside of the empire: being the support of the Church one of the pillars of his internal policy, a divided church would have meant a weakening also of his own personal power and, possibly, a further division of the empire itself into arrays disrupting the unity which was his final goal.

Unluckily, the IV century Church was living a difficult period due to the lack of a fully and universally recognized doctrine and of a fully and universally recognized structure of power[121]. We have already analyzed the interventions of Constantine against the Donatists: that was surely an hard crisis, but finally quite limited both in numerical and geographical terms. Possibly even harder was the new problem which was looming against the Church unity: this time Arianism was the crisis and Arius the one who provoked it, and both had a long backgroung that needs to be seen not to risk to lose the full meaning of Nicea[122]. The beginnings of Arianism may be traced very far, to the writings of Philo (20 B.C. to A.D.50), the Jewish thinker and exegete who exercised a strong influence on many Christian interpreters of the Scriptures. Philo's main achievement was his development of the allegorical interpretation of the Bible, which enabled him to find much of Greek philosophy in the Old Testament, and to combine respect of his religion for the Pentateuch with his own penchant for a more spiritual understanding of the Word of God. He accorded a central place in his system to the "Logos", who was at once the creative power that orders the world and the intermediary through whom men can know God. The Logos was the one who spoke to Moses in the burning bush, and who is represented in the Old Testament under the figure of a high priest. His influence was particularly great in the Alexandrine school of Christian theology. Clement of Alexandria and Origen used him freely, and through them and later through some Latin Fathers, his allegorical exegesis became a standard form of Bible study in the Church. Unfortunately for the Church, Philo's concept of a created medium between God and man entered religious history

---

121) B.D.Ehrman, *Lost Christianities: The Battles for Scripture and the Faiths We Never Knew*, Oxford University Press, 2005, p.21
122) In tracing the routes of Arianism: R.Williams, *Arius: Heresy and Tradition*, Wm. B. Eerdmans Publishing Company, 2002, passim and J.O'Grady, *Early Christian Heresies*, New Ed. Edition, 1995, passim

to confuse the mainstream of Christian thought and was later brought to the extreme consequences by some currents of the Gnosticism. As we know, Gnosticism was a complex religious movement which, in some of its branches denied the historical validity of the Gospels. Christ, they said, was not the Deity in human form but only an "aeon", or intermediary, who was apparently endowed with human nature. Accordingly, salvation was not to be obtained through the merits of Christ, but through the Gnosis or superior knowledge which was manifested in Him and discovered by the Gnostics. Christ, therefore, was not really born, nor did He actually live and die or rise from the grave. The events described in the Gospels were not historically but only symbolically true. Spiritual insight, possessed by the Gnostics, and not the reported words and deeds of Christ, furnished Christianity with the religious truths of salvation. Many Fathers combated Gnosticism and outstanding among them was Ireneus (A.D.130-200), Bishop of Lyons who, in his chief work, *Against the Heresies*, made a detailed exposé of Gnosticism. Although Gnosticism was disposed of in practice, its theories were actually never far from the boundaries of the faith. Where believing Christians were willing to follow Ireneus and the other Fathers and accept the Church's teaching about Christ, as the bishops and popes proclaimed it, sophisticated intellectuals were less easily satisfied and their speculations continued unhindered (albeit rejected) throughout the III century.

Less well known than Gnosticism, Manichaeism had a corresponding effect on Christian tradition and did much to stimulate the rise of Arianism. In Manichaean theory, in fact, man was indeed created by God with pure elements, but he was made a prisoner by Satan who planted in him the seeds of darkness. Since that time, man has become the subject of a struggle between God and the evil Spirit. The only hope for man is by the practice of severe asceticism, which comprises the three seals or mortifications of the mouth, the hands, and the passions. The followers of Manes developed his main ideas to which they added Gnostic speculations, claiming, as the Gnostics did, to a special gnosis or divine insight. They explained the dualism they had inherited from Zoroastrianism by saying that from the good principle there emanated, in the first place, the primeval man, who was the first to enter into the struggle with evil; in the next place the Spirit of Life, who rescued the primeval man from the powers of darkness; finally the World-Soul, Christ, the Son of the primeval man, who restored to men the light they had lost in the conflict with darkness. They distinguished in man two souls, the soul that animates the body, and the soul of light, which is part of the World-Soul, Christ. The former is the creation of the powers of darkness, the latter is an emanation from the light itself. Thus, man's soul is a battlefield on which light and darkness are at war, as they are in the universe at large. Human action depends on the outcome of the contest; there is no freedom of choice. All material things are evil and the cause of evil. Manichaean influence on Arianism gave it the main premise for its teaching. If, on Manichaean grounds, the body is evil, God could not have become man because the Holy One cannot deny His nature to form one personality with sin.

If the foregoing may be considered remote precursors of Arianism, as giving the climate for its rise, the real roots must be, anyway, traced to four men whose names have become attached to their respective systems of thought: Montanus, Sabellius, Paul of Samosata, and Lucian of Antioch.

According to Montanus, whose heresy we already mentioned, at the Last Supper, Jesus had foretold the coming of the Paraclete and these promises were being realized in him. So Montanus was the Paraclete even as Christ was the Son of God, who, according to the heretic, would soon return to earth and found a New Jerusalem: this equating of divine filiation in Christ with the divine procession of Montanus lowered the concept of Christ's divinity to a sort of metaphor[123]. But early in the III century a more formidable challenge arose in the person of Sabellius, who wrote around A.D. 215 and developed what has since become known as Modalist Monarchianism. As a general premise, Monarchianism sought to safeguard Monotheism and the Unity (Monarchy) of the Godhead. But the movement slipped into heresy because it failed to do justice to the independent subsistence of the Son. Sabellianism or Modalist Monarchianism, taught that in the Godhead the only differentiation was a mere succession of modes or operations. The Sabellianists were also called "Patripassians", since it was a corollary of their doctrine that the Father suffered as the Son.

The father of "Adoptionist Monarchianism", or at least its most famous proponent, was Paul of Samosata, former Bishop of Antioch, deposed in A.D. 268 for his heretical teaching. Along with Theodotus and Artemon, he maintained that Jesus was God only in the sense that a special power or influence rested upon His human person: his Christological thesis was that from the incarnation the Logos rested upon the human Jesus as one person upon another, and that the incarnate Christ differed only in degree from the ancient prophets.

It is commonly believed that Paul of Samosata was the teacher of Lucian of Antioch, who died in A.D. 312 and who was certainly the most influential factor in Arius' theology, so much that the Arians prided themselves on being Lucianists.

Lucian was a priest and theologian, who founded an important school of learning where Arius and Eusebius of Nicomedia were students. In Christology, he professed a form of "Subordinationism" that later became known as "Semi-Arianism". For some time he was excommunicated for heterodoxy, but ten years or so before martyrdom, he was

---

123) *Ibidem*, pp. 164-181

reconciled to the Church, and we may suppose retracted his earlier theories[124].

So, we come to Arius. Authorities[125] differ about the details of his life. He was probably a Libyan by birth (A.D. 250), had been a pupil of Lucian, and been ordained deacon by Peter, Bishop of Alexandria (before A.D. 312), who later excommunicated him as a member of the Donatist sect.

Under Achillas (A.D. 312-313), Peter's successor, he was ordained priest and put in charge of Baucalis, one of the main churches of Alexandria. A man known for his asceticism and fine preaching, Arius became (about A.D.319) a champion of the "Subordinationist Theory" (thinking that Christ was not equal but subordinate to the Father). The controversy aroused has made history: Arius rallied to his support a number of prominent Lucianists, particularly Eusebius of Nicomedia, while a synod at Alexandria (A.D. 320-321) was summoned by the new bishop, Alexander, who excommunicated Arius[126].

One could think about a sort of "simple" theological quarrel, totally internal to the high and cultured ranks of the church, but to think this one should forget that the whole church, just shaken by many other disputes and heresies, was very sensible, at all levels, to any new Christological idea and that, although not having a great sequel inside of the Catholic clergy, the opinions of Arius had a strong influence on the intellectual circles of Alexandria and, being Alexandria one of the most important centers of Christian thought in the Roman empire, that meant to have a strong influence on the whole

---

124) In relation to the evolutions of the "Antioch School": J.Lebreton, *Heresy and Orthodoxy (A History of the Early Church)*, Collier Books, 1962, pp. 194-232

125) Here we follow the version by Epiphanius (Epiphanius of Salamis, *Panarion*, LIX)

126) H.M. Gwatkin, *The Arian Controversy*, BiblioBazaar, 2007, p.74

Christianity[127].

Constantine, informed of the dispute, once again tried to intervene directly, counting on the weight of his still unformalized but surely strong role of Church patron and, quite evidently forecasting a much deeper trouble in respect to the one faced with the Donatist heresy, immediately after the council wrote on his own initiative a joint letter to Arius and his bishop Alexander, urging them to give up their quarrel and come to terms in the interests of peace in the Alexandrian territory. Characteristically, Constantine, once more showing no direct interest in the light theological disputes of his allies but underlining the political interest of his patronage, gave two reasons for writing to them: his desire to have one single religion in the empire, as a guarantee of political unity, and his fear that theological wrangling over points of doctrine could weaken the civil institutions of the land[128]. Here is the content of his missive, as reported by Eusebius: *"On investigation, I find that the reason for this quarrel is insignificant and worthless. As I understand it, you, Alexander, were asking the separate opinions of your clergy on some passage of your law, or rather were inquiring about some idle question, when you, Arius, inconsistently committed yourself to statements which should either never have come to your mind, or have been at once repressed. Your contention is not about any fundamental issue of your law. Neither of you is introducing any novel scheme of worship. You are of one and the same way of thinking, so that it is in your power to unite in one communion. Even philosophers can agree together, one and all, on one principle, though differing in particulars. Is it right for brothers to oppose brothers for the sake of trifles? Such conduct might be expected from the uncultured, or from the recklessness of boys. But it is little in keeping*

---

127) R.P.C. Hanson, *The Search for the Christian Doctrine of God: The Arian Controversy, 318-381*, Baker Academic, 2006, pp.321-322
128) M. Wiles, *Archetypal Heresy: Arianism through the Centuries*, Oxford University Press, 2001, pp. 111-114

with your sacred profession and with your personal wisdom."[129]

Under pressure from the emperor to make up and forget about their "trifles", and from bishop Alexander to retract their unorthodox teaching, the Arians defended themselves by writing a letter of explanation to Alexander. We must remember that, by this time, they had already been condemned in the Synod of Egypt, so that the letter can be read as a "considered and conciliatory statement" before the condemnation as well as a sarcastic defiance, more likely to have followed it.

For a long time, as stated by Hilary of Poitiers[130], this text served as a formalized Arian Confession and we can read it as reported by Athanasius[131] and Epiphanius[132]. "*To our blessed pope and bishop Alexander the presbyters and deacons send greeting in the Lord. Our faith which we received from our forefathers and have also learned from you is this. We know there is one God, the only unbegotten, only eternal, only without beginning, only true, who only has immortality, only wise, only good, the only potentate, judge of all, governor, dispenser, unalterable and unchangeable, righteous and good, God of the Law and the prophets and the New Covenant. Before everlasting ages he begot his unique Son, through whom he made the ages and all things. He begot him not in appearance, but in truth, constituting him by his own will, unalterable and unchangeable, a perfect creature of God, but not as one of the creatures--an offspring, but not as one of things begotten. Neither* [was] *the offspring of the Father a projection, as Valentinus taught, nor, as Manichaeus introduced, was the offspring a consubstantial part of the Father, nor* [was he], *as Sabellius said, dividing the Monad, a Son-Father, nor, as Hieracas* [taught], *a lamp* [kindled] *from a lamp, or like a torch* [divided] *into two, nor did he first exist, later being begotten or re-created into a Son--as you also, blessed pope, in the midst of the Church and in council often refuted those who introduced these* [ideas]. *But as we said, by the will of*

---

129) Eusebius of Caesarea, *Vita Constantini*, II, 64-72
130) Hilary of Poitiers, *De Trinitate*, IV, 12
131) Athanasius of Alexandria, *De Concilii*, XVI
132) Epiphanius of Salamis, *Cit.*, LIX.7

God [he was] *created before times and before ages and received life and being and glories from the Father, the Father so constituting him. Nor did the Father in giving him the inheritance of all things deprived himself of what he possesses unbegottenly in himself, for he is the fount of all things. Thus there are three hypostases. God being the cause of all things is without beginning and most unique, while the Son, begotten timelessly by the Father and created before ages and established, was not before he was begotten--but, begotten timelessly before all things, he alone was constituted by the Father. He is neither eternal nor coeternal nor co-unbegotten with the Father, nor does he have his being together with the Father, as some say 'others with one', introducing* [the idea of] *two unbegotten sources. But as Monad and cause of all, God is thus before all. Therefore he is also prior to the Son, as we learned from what you preached in the midst of the Church. So therefore, as he has being and glories from God, and life and all things were given him, accordingly God is his source. For he precedes him as his God, and as being before him. But if the* [phrases] *'of him' and 'out of the womb' and 'I came forth from the Father and am come'* [133] *are understood by some as* [meaning] *a part of the consubstantial himself and a projection, then according to them the Father is compound and divisible and alterable and a body, and according to them presumably, the bodiless God* [is thought of as] *suffering what belongs to a body. We pray that you may fare well in the Lord, blessed pope. Arius, Aeithales, Achilleus, Carpones, Sarmatas, Arius, presbyters. Deacons, Euzoius, Lucius, Julius, Menas, Helladius, Gaius. Bishops, Secundus of Pentapolis, Theonas of Libya, Pistus (whom the Arians installed at Alexandria)*[134].*"*

---

133) Respectively Rom. 11:36; Ps. 110:3; John 8:42; 16:28

134) The signatures are preserved only by Epiphanius. The two Arian bishops Secundus and Theonas were deposed by the Egyptian Synod and again at Nicea. Pistus doubtless added his signature to this document later, when he was consecrated by Secundus as a claimant to the see of Alexandria, where an effort was made to install him in A.D. 338-339 (Athanasius, *Defense Against the Arians*, XXIV). He may have signed as bishop of Alexandria, for which an orthodox transmitter of the letter substituted the explanatory note now found at the end. The other signatures look as if each presbyter were supported by his deacon; Eusebius

The date of this letter is about 320 A.D., and reveals a number of salient features of Arianism, besides the obvious fact that Arius and his followers were unimpressed by Constantine's criticism that this was not a matter of crucial importance to Christianity. In the Arian confession to Alexander, the pivotal word is eternal, since it was the denial of the Son's eternity with the Father that lay at the basis of Arian heterodoxy and, at Nicea, as we will see, proved to be the test which the council used against them[135].

The joint letter to Alexander should be read together with another communication from Arius himself, written about the same time, to his friend, Bishop Eusebius of Nicomedia. Eusebius had just been transferred from the See of Berytus in Syria to that of the imperial residence, Nicomedia. It gives us a more frank statement of Arius' position as he was willing to express it to his friends.

"To my very dear lord, the faithful and orthodox man of God Eusebius, Arius, unjustly persecuted by Pope Alexander for the sake of the all-conquering truth of which you also are a defender, sends greetings in the Lord. Since my father Ammonius was coming to Nicomedia, it seemed to me fitting and proper to send greetings by him, and also to bring to your attention, in the natural love and affection which you have for the brethren, for the sake of God and his Christ, that the bishop greatly injures and persecutes us and does all he can against us, trying to drive us out of the city as godless men, since we do not agree with him when he says publicly, 'Always Father, always Son', 'Father and Son together', 'The Son exists unbegottenly with God, the eternal begotten'. What is it that we say, and think, and have taught, and teach? That the Son is not unbegotten, nor a part of the unbegotten in any way, nor formed out of any substratum, but that he was constituted by God's will and counsel, before times and before

---

remained closely associated with Arius, and survived to be Arian bishop of Antioch from A.D. 361 to A.D. 378.
135) M.Wiles, *Cit.*, p.123

ages, full (of grace and truth), divine, unique, unchangeable. And before he was begotten or created or ordained or founded, he was not. For he was not unbegotten. We are persecuted because we say, 'The Son has a beginning, but God is without beginning'. For this we are persecuted, and because we say, 'He is made out of things that were not'. But this is what we say, since he is neither part of God nor formed out of any substratum. For this we are persecuted, and you know the rest."[136]

Looking back at the Arian position, we can think it is rather rational, as may distinguish two elements that constitute the idea of sonship in ordinary human relations: a son does not exist before he is born and a son has the same nature as his father. The main argument of the Arians was that Christ was a Son, and therefore was not eternal, but of a substance which had a beginning. For this reason Arius, in his debate with Alexander, urged that: "*If the Father begot the Son, he that was begotten had a beginning of existence. From this it is plain that once the son was not, and it follows of necessity that he had his subsistence out of nothing*". In what sense, then, is sonship to be attributed to the divine nature of Christ? Catholic tradition before Arius said that the true meaning of the word was "consubstantiality" (co-essentiality) with the Father, whereas the point of subsequentness to the Father depended on time, which we cannot attribute to God. But the Arians insisted that a son has his origin of existence from his father: what has an origin has a beginning; what has a beginning is not from eternity; what is not from eternity is not from God. Therefore, they refused to admit that origination and beginning are not necessarily convertible terms: in other words, they would not allow that anything can have an origin and not have a beginning. They further claimed that a son not only has his origin of existence from his father, but also his nature, and all that is proper to his nature, and therefore in the absolute sense, is dependent on the father), as effect depends on its

---

136) Reported in Eusebius of Caesarea, *Cit.*.

cause. They went on to say that if you maintain God has a true son, you are blaspheming because you imply in God a division of substance (as happens in bodily generation), and change (since a human father acquires a son he did not have before), and composition (for human procreation is possible only because the parent is composed of body, which he reproduces, and of soul which cannot be transfused). If we must admit, argued the Arians, that in some sense Christ is son of God, it can only be as one who is numerically distinct from God, inferior to God by reason of dependence and time, and consequently a creature but not absolutely equally God. Sonship then becomes a quality or characteristic bestowed on a creature (a sort of adjective added to a contingent being), but not a substantive that pertains to the very existence of God by a necessity of essence[137].

Unexpectedly, however, while the Arians were unwilling to allow that Jesus Christ was Son by nature, and maintained that the word implied a beginning of existence, they would not say that He was Son merely in the same way that we are sons of God. Athanasius was to push their premises to their conclusion, and pressed them to explain how the Savior was at the same time a creature and yet not as one of the creatures[138].

Under pressure, also as Constantine, with his letter, had sent to Alexandria also one of his most faithful and influent advisors, that Hosius of Cordoba who someone sees as the converter of the emperor[139] (which is doubtful) and who, anyway, was considered one of the harder moral censors of the

---

137) For an explanation of the Arian theories: R.C. Gregg, *Arianism: Historical and Theological Reassessments: Papers from the Ninth International Conference on Patristic Studies*,Wipf & Stock Publishers, 2006, passim
138) Athanasius of Alexandria, *Orations Against the Arians*, II
139) F.J. Zrodowski, *The concept of Heresy According to Cardinal Hosius*,The Catholic university of America press, 1947, pp.12-13

Christianity[140], to arbitrate the dispute, the Arians[141] devised a more refined argument. They abandoned the question of time and the analysis of the word son. Instead they urged that, no matter how you consider the relation of Father and Son, you always imply a voluntary originator (since a human father freely wills to beget), and a free gift conferred (since the child need not have been born). Their argument was reduced to the dilemma: "Did the Father give birth to the Son willingly or unwillingly?" They were in turn, asked: "Is the Father true God willingly or unwillingly?"[142] In Athanasius' words: *"The Arians direct their view to the contradictory of willing, instead of looking at the more important and prior question: as much as unwillingness is opposed to willing, so is nature prior to willing, and leads the way to it."*[143] In other words, the real issue is not to argue backwards from human generation, which is certainly a free act; but to ask if God is by nature Triune, so that He necessarily begets a Son, and would not be God were He not Father and Son (and also Spirit).

To this extent and while the ideas of Arius were rapidly spreading far beyond the area of Alexandria and the one of Antioch, touching, probably thanks to the predication of Eusebius of Nicomedia, also the imperial environment, Hosius went back to the emperor and most probably suggested him that he needed to act immediately to eradicate the heresy as soon as possible. It's difficult to speculate about the position of Constantine: on one side, Hosius was very close to him, on the

---

140) In particular with his severe canons, expressed in the council of Illiberis or Elvira, concerning such points of discipline as the treatment of those who had abjured their faith during the recent persecutions and questions concerning clerical marriage.
141) Arius, *Confession to Constantine* (as recorded in Socrates, *Church History*,1.26.2 and Sozomen, *Church History*, 2.27.6-10)
142) W.H.Carroll, *The Revolution Against Christendom: A History of Christendom*, Vol. 5, Christendom Press, 2006, p.131
143) Athanasius of Alexandria, History of the Arians,V

other, also Eusebius was (so much that we have seen him as presumed baptizer of the emperor before his death). It is probable that Constantine was completely neutral about the terms of the quarrel, but, as before noted, he was deeply interested in the unity of Christianity and surely Arianism was a threat (actually not the only one as aftereffects of previous contrasts were still present here and there) in that sense[144].

The imperial solution was, therefore, to let the experts discuss about theology in a council whose goal had to be formally only one, unity, but which could also be useful to strengthen his position towards Christianity.

The council projected for this purpose passed to history with the name of its host town: Nicea.

---

144) H.A. Drake, *Constantine and the Bishops: The Politics of Intolerance*, The Johns Hopkins University Press, 2002, p.27-29

II.2) THE CALL FOR NICEA

At the very beginning, when Hosius was given by Constantine the organization of the council, the idea was to hold it in Ancyra[145] (modern Ankara) as it seemed to be the best place to reckon bishops from both parts of the empire, East and West. Just since this moment the council was, in fact, meant to be really "ecumenical"[146]. This gives us the possibility to reflect about the sense of this meeting of "all Christianity" on Constantine point of view.

It's absolutely true that the Arian heresy was for sure a theologically hard one for the Church and, therefore, for the imperial unity and that the ideas of Arius were spreading rapidly but, on the other hand, other matters more or less of the same gravity had, till that moment, been discussed only locally or, at least, enlarging the meeting, as in Alexandria, only to the nearby areas. So, why to organize an ecumenical council for Arius? Let's forget for a moment about the theological problems (we already know that they were surely of minor importance for an emperor not even understanding them completely and even dithering about which position was correct in relation to the the counselor he was speaking with) and analyze the whole thing politically. Focusing on the role of Constantine it is quite clear that the Arian controversy was a wonderful opportunity to show to the whole Christianity his position of Church protector and, somehow, to formalize it, showing his magnificence and

---

145) R.Algheimer, *The council of Nicea*, Preston Press, 2001, p.34
146) Ecumenical, from Koine Greek "oikoumenikos", literally meaning worldwide but generally assumed to be limited to the Roman empire as in Augustus' claim to be ruler of the oikoumene/world; the earliest extant uses of the term for a council are Eusebius' *Life of Constantine* 3.6 around 338, Athanasius' *Ad Afros Epistola Synodica* in 369, and the *Letter* in 382 to Pope Damasus I and the Latin bishops from the First council of Constantinople

goodwill and, therefore, ratifying the existent in front of the maximum Christian authorities. It's possibly not without a sense that the whole organization came directly from the imperial palace and that the council was coincident with the great celebrations for the XX anniversary of the accession of the emperor to the throne, taking place just immediately after the council, with the obvious participation of many council fathers: it's another confirmation of the strict relation Constantine wanted to state between himself and the Christian population.

Was the council organization arranged with the pope? Actually we don't know and scholars have different opinions. Someone[147] think that the non-appearance of pope Sylvester to the council (sending only two priests to represent the Roman See) was an act of undeclared protest against the lack of previous communication of the council from Nicomedia and, practically, the exclusion of Rome from the organization. It's a quite questionable thesis: in reality, although surely not as tight as stated in some legendary accounts such as the *Vita Beati Sylvestri*[148], a strong relation between the emperor and the pope is practically sure[149] and it would have been politically rather stupid by Constantine to exclude pope Sylvester from the organization, at least preventively informing him. The lack of presence of the pope was most possibly due effectively to his late age[150] and the two legates he sent, although being only priests, were, anyway, members of the pope's court and his

---

147) In example L.Lewys, *Constantine and the Church: Strategy of a Difficult Marriage*, Absalom, 2004, pp. 97-109

148) *Vita Beati Sylvestri*, reported in J.P.N. Land, *Anecdota Syriaca*, III, Leiden 1889, 46ff. and in L.Surius, *Vitae Sanctorum*, VI, Cologne, 1617, 1173ff

149) L.Lewys, *Cit.*, p.82

150) We don't know his birth date but, having become pope in A.D. 314 we can imagine he was at least 65 or 70, which meant a quite old age for the period.

close advisors[151].

To affirm his presence not only "in spiritu" but also physically, in spring A.D.325 Constantine changed his plans radically and moved the seat of the council as close as possible to his official residence in Nicomedia (to move it directly to Nicomedia would have been problematic, openly showing a too direct control on the council events and also giving the bishops in the hands of a town directly controlled, through Eusebius of Nicomedia, by the Arians).

Nicea (modern Iznik in Turkey) was the perfect seat for such an important meeting. Founded in the 4th century B.C. by the Macedonian king Antigonus I Monophthalmus, geographically it was about 30 miles far from the Sea of Marmara, located at the East end of the Iznik or Nicean Lake, in the heart of the Nicean Valley, one of earth's most botanically luxurious and simply beautiful valleys of the Middle East. The climate was mild all year long and the area was also on an important crossroads between Galatia and Phrygia, and thus saw steady trade and easy communications. But, most important of all, in Nicea Constantine had a big, wonderful palace, built inside of the famous city fortress, whose huge and imposing walls were famous for their security and Nicea was only a few miles from the imperial seat of Nicomedia, so that it could be reached in less than an hour ride. Definitely, if the emperor wanted to be present at the council and, at the same time to offer a luxurious, comfortable and safe place to the fathers, a place able to impress them and to show them his power, Nicea was the right choice[152]. And also the Arian tendency (although not as extreme as in Nicomedia) of the population could be a great help in showing the imperial power.

---

151) I.Ortiz de Urbina, *Storia dei concili ecumenici. Vol. 1: Nicea e Costantinopoli*, Libreria Editrice Vaticana 1994, p.77

152) R. Attworth, *Nicea: the Council that Changed Christianity*, Best Value Publishing House, 1997, pp.38-44

The idea to give a comfortable seat to the council fathers was, actually, only a part of a wilder strategy by Constantine to favor the church leaders goodwill. We don't have to forget that imperial persecutions, mainly for the Eastern bishops, were just behind their shoulders (many of them were still suffering for the consequences of imprisonments and tortures) and the building of a new trust was not an easy job for the emperor.

This is most probably the reason of a kindness and a treatment which had very few precedents in the history of the Roman relations, starting since the tone of the convocation.

About 1800 copies of the invitation to the council were sent from the Nicomedia palace through imperial emissaries to all the dioceses at the four corners of the empire.

We could have a big part of the text thanks to a Syrian manuscript dated A.D.501, although it's quite doubtful it reports the exact text of the convocation, recorded by Eusebius[153]:

"That there is nothing more honorable in my sight than the fear of God, I believe is manifest to every man. Now, because the Synod of Bishops at Ancyra, of Galatia, consented at first that it should be, it now seems on many accounts that it would be well for a Synod to assemble at Nicea, a city of Bithynia, both because the Bishops of Italy and the rest of the countries of Europe are coming, and also because of the excellent temperature of the air, and also because I shall be present as a spectator and participator of what is done. Wherefore I signify to you, my beloved brethren, that I earnestly wish all of yon to assemble at this city which is named, that is at Nicea. Let every one of you therefore, considering that which is best, as I before said, be diligent without any delay speedily to come, that he may be present in his own person as a spectator of what is done. God keep you, my beloved brethren."[154]

There seems to be no reason to doubt about the conditions of

---

153) Eusebius of Caesarea, *Vita*, Cit. , III
154) B. H. Cowper, *Syriac Miscellanies, The council Of Nicea. Extracts From The Codex Syriacus 38 In The Imperial Library At Paris*, Williams and Norgate, 1861, p.249

travel offered to the bishops and recorded, once again, by Eusebius[155]. Constantine put the imperial transportation system at disposal of the bishops. This meant they could travel on his boats free, that they could go by cart, wagon, horse or whatever means the empire had to offer, all under the protection of the Roman army (travel was not only difficult, but also dangerous). Constantine housed the bishops, fed them and provided his own palace as a place to meet.

Unluckily, it was not a good time for traveling. The Eastern rivers were flooded with the rains of a late spring, and although the empire, stretching from Britain to the borders of Persia, was nominally at peace, there were marauding soldiers and bandits along the roads. Moreover, we can imagine that not all trusted in an imperial power which had fought them so harshly till a few years before. So, of the 1000 bishops invited from the East and the 800 from the West, less than 350 bishops answered the imperial summons. Their exact number is actually discussed: Eusebius of Caesarea counted 250[156], Athanasius of Alexandria counted 318[157], and Eustathius of Antioch counted 270[158] (all three were present at the council). Later, Socrates Scholasticus recorded more than 300[159], and Hilarius[160] and Jerome[161] again 318, which became the official historical number of the participants, although this may be a symbolic element representing the 318 servants of Abraham[162].

Actually, their numbers were swelled by a horde of attendant presbyters, deacons, sub deacons, and laymen, as, although each

---

155) Eusebius of Caesarea, *Cit.*, III
156) *Ibidem*, III.9
157) Athanasius of Alexandria, *Ad Afros Epistola Synodica*, II
158) Reported by Theodoret, *Historia Ecclesiae*, I.8
159) Socrates Scholasticus, *Historia Ecclesiae*, IX
160) Hilary of Poitiers, *Contra Constantium*, I
161) Jerome, *Chronicon*, IV
162) Gen. 14:14

one had permission to bring with him only two priests and three deacons, this order, according to Eusebius[163], was respected by no one.

Most of the ecclesiastics came from the East, both for a matter of distances and as Europe and North Africa had not yet been corrupted by the schism.

Only six bishops and two presbyters represented the West. They were Hosius of Cordova, the real organizer of the council, Caecilian of Carthage, Nicasius of Dijon, Domnus of Strido in Pannonia, Eustorgius of Milan, and Marcus of Calabria. The two Roman presbyters Victor and Vincentius represented the old Sylvester, bishop of Rome.

Many of the bishops who came from the East had suffered persecution. There was Paul, bishop of Mesopotamian Caesarea, with his hands scorched by flames; Paphnutius of Upper Egypt, famous for the austerity of his life, had had his right eye dug out and the sinews of his left leg cut during the Diocletian persecution; Potammon of Heraclea, who had known Anthony and lived in the deserts of the Nile, had also lost an eye; there was Jacob, bishop of Nisibis, who, being a former hermit, wore a coat of camel hair; from the island of Cyprus came Bishop Spyridion, a saintly shepherd who refused to give up tending sheep even when he was elevated to the episcopate, a man who performed miracles to the delight of the Cypriots and was famous mainly for his thundering against virginity. The first rank was held by the three patriarchs: Alexander of Alexandria, Eustathius of Antioch and Macarius of Jerusalem, but among the other remarkable attendees we can remember Nicholas of Myra, Aristakes of Armenia (son of Saint Gregory the Illuminator), Leontius of Caesarea, Hypatius of Granga, Protogenes of Sardica, Melitius of Sebastopolis; Achilleus of Larissa and Athanasius of Thessaly.

---

163) Eusebius of Caesarea, *Cit.*

Three bishops had arrived even from outside of the empire: the Persian bishop John, the Gothic bishop Theophilus and Stratophilus, bishop of Pitiunt in Egrisi (located at the border of modern-day Russia and Georgia).
The supporters of Arius included Secundus of Ptolemais, Theonus of Marmarica, Zephyrius, and Dathes, all of whom hailed from Libya and the Pentapolis, the famous Eusebius of Nicomedia and Eusebius of Caesarea, Paulinus of Tyrus, Actius of Lydda, Menophantus of Ephesus, and Theognus of Nicaea[164].
This motley crew of bishops represented varying traditions of Christianity. There were sharp-featured intellectuals, men of abstruse book learning, capable of splitting hairs by the yard. There were wise old hermits who had spent the previous year clothed in rough goat hair cloaks, living on roots and leaves. There were men so saintly that it was almost expected of them that they would perform miracles during the council. There were cantankerous men, and men riddled with heresies, and men who rode to Nicea in hope of preferment from the hands of the emperor. There were men who came peacefully, intending only to observe and then report to their flock, and there were other men determined to wage war in the council chamber[165].
Even if only "in epitome", with much less participants than Constantine had expected, somehow the whole Christianity (perhaps with the only exception of the Britannic believers) was present under the presidency of Hosius and the supervision of Constantine when, in that spring of A.D. 325 the first Ecumenic council of the history of Christianity started.

---

164) For a list of the participants, in majority derived from the accounts of Athanasius and Eusebius, R.E. Rubenstein, *When Jesus Became God: The Struggle to Define Christianity during the Last Days of Rome*, Harvest Books, 2000, pp.88ff
165) R. Attworth, *Cit.*, pp. 63-64

Dr. Lawrence M.F. Sudbury – **Nicea: what it was, what it was not**

II.3) WHAT WE HISTORICALLY KNOW

Influenced by more recent councils (from the V Lateran council with its five years to the council of Trent with its 18 years, although not continuous, to the II Vatican council with its three years), one could think that the council Of Nicea was a long business. Actually, it lasted only a couple of months and the real clue moment, related to the discussion of the Arian theories, not more than a few days. Although there isn't a total agreement among early authorities as to the month and day of the opening, in order to reconcile the indications furnished by Socrates[166] and by the *Acts of the council of Chalcedon*[167], this date may, perhaps, be taken as May 20th : it may be assumed without too great hardihood that the synod, having been convoked for May 20th, in the absence of the emperor held meetings of a less solemn character until June 14th, when, after the emperor's arrival, the real official discussion started and lasted up to June 19th, after which various matters of minor importance were dealt with, and the sessions came to an end on August 25th.

As already stated, many writers gave us different versions of the works of the real council (the one starting on June 14th) but we don't have any kind of official acts transcript, so that the only thing we can try to do is to recollect all the different accounts of Eusebius[168], Athanasius[169], Socrates[170], Sozomen[171], Hilarius[172] and all the (later) others and draw a sort of chronologically judicious account of the events.

Before proceeding, anyway, it is useful to briefly analyze the role

---

166) Socrates Scholasticus, *Historia Ecclesiae*, V
167) AA.VV., *Acts of the Council of Chalcedon*, II
168) Eusebius of Caesarea, *Cit.*
169) Athanasius, *Cit.*
170) Socrates Scolasticus, *Cit.*
171) Sozomen, *Cit.*
172) Hilary of Poitiers, *Cit.*

Constantine had in the decisions taken during this synod and the freedom left to the council fathers. As to the second point, Eusebius ensures us that *"...detachments of the body-guard and troops surrounded the entrance of the palace with drawn swords, and through the midst of them the men of God proceeded without fear into the innermost of the Imperial apartments..."*[173], so that, although the book of this father is often more similar to a panegyric of Constantine than to a biography, we are informed (and, not being the use of the imperial army to guard a religious council particularly commendatory in term of liberty for Constantine, we can easily believe) that the Synod was rather protected from any possible external influence. The terms are quite different in relation to the first point. Fundamentally, the question is: how much Constantine ideas interfered with the decision of the Christian fathers? Once again Eusebius tells us that the session was frequently honored by the presence of the emperor, who used to seat (with the permission of the council) on a low stool in the midst of the hall, *"to listened with patience, and speak with modesty"* and who, in at least one occasion *"humbly professed that he was the minister, not the judge, of the successors of the apostles, who had been established as priests and as gods upon earth."*[174] Unluckily we already know that the source of such a description is strongly partisan and therefore not completely deserving our trust. As a matter of fact, Constantine had a strong role: he was not only a sort of honorary president of the assembly and the amphitryon of all the participants, but also the one having the last word about all the decisions (in particular, as we will see, in relation to the creed). We already know he was not particularly (not to say at all) interested in theological disquisitions and it is possibly in this sense, as also Athanasius[175] assures, that the activities of the

---

173) Eusebius, *Vita*, III.15
174) Eusebius, *Cit.*, VII
175) Athanasius, *Letter Concerning the Decrees of the council of Nicaea (De Decretis)*, II

council were not hampered by Constantine's presence. Surely, anyway, the emperor had, by that time, escaped from the influence of Eusebius of Nicomedia and was under that of Hosius, to whom, as well as to Athanasius himself, may be attributed a preponderant influence in the formulation of the symbol. Therefore, we can't exclude that, although indirectly (and quite surely without any form of personal and mainly physical pressure), the favor of Constantine towards one of the leaders of the so-called "orthodox array"(and his will, by the way, to favor the most rooted position in Christianity to recompose a politically fitting unity) may have, somehow, doped the final results of the council.

It's, moreover, not without a sense that the real council started only with the arrival of Constantine and the strength of his presence (even if he never voted) shines through the relations of all the writers reporting the moment of his entrance.

Eusebius enthusiastically wrote *"himself proceeded through the midst of the assembly, like some heavenly messenger of God, clothed in raiment which glittered as it were with rays of light, reflecting the glowing radiance of a purple robe, and adorned with the brilliant splendor of gold and precious stones"*[176], but even without reaching this points of adulation, putting together the different relations we get a picture of great solemnity. The emperor waited until all the bishops had taken their seats before making his entry. He was clad in gold and covered with precious stones in the fashion of an Oriental sovereign. A chair of gold had been made ready for him, and when he had taken his place the bishops seated themselves. Sozomen[177] attempts to give a sort of visual impression of the emperor, saying that he was then fifty-one but looked younger, enormously tall and vigorous, with a high color and a strange glitter in his fierce, lion-like eyes. He wore

---

176) Eusebius, *Cit.*, III.10
177) Sozomen, *Cit.*, II

his hair long, but his beard was trimmed short. He had a thick heavy neck and a curious way of holding his head back, so that it seemed not to be well set on the powerful shoulders, and there was about all his movements a remarkable casualness, so that when he strode, he gave the impression of someone dancing. Is it possible that even the most objective council father was not at least touched by the presence of such a figure, introduced in the assembly in such a spectacular ostentation of power?

Actually, even if the formal president of the assembly was Hosius of Cordova, assisted by the pope's legates, Victor and Vincentius, who was the real leader there? The whole chronology of the events of the opening sitting answers to this question and, once again it's worth repeating it, gives us the real sense of the council, at least in Constantine's intentions: he was the power, he was the protector of Christianity, he was the center around which Christianity had to grow.

First of all Constantine spent some time accepting scrolls (secret petitions for favors and for redress) from the many bishops in attendance, then the Bishop Eusebius of Caesarea (or, more likely, Eustathius of Antioch[178]) read a speech of welcome in metrical prose and then chanted a hymn of thanksgiving for the emperor's victories; finally, once again there was silence.

At this moment, Constantine collected himself, and speaking in Latin, which was still the language of the court, in a voice that seemed strangely soft and gentle for such a commanding man[179], he bade the bishops remember that it was the power of God that had dethroned the tyrants, and worse than any battlefield was a civil war between factions of the church. *"It is my desire,"* he said, *"that you should meet together in a general council,*

---

178) The thing is discussed and both are mentioned by different authors
179) Sozomen, *Cit.*, II

and so I offer to the King of All my gratitude for this mercy that has come to me above my other mercies. I mean that there has been granted to me the benefit of seeing you assembled together and to know you are resolved to be in common harmony together." All this was flattery, for the very purpose of the convocation was, formally, to resolve a bitter conflict, and Constantine knew well enough from the many petitions he had already received before the council from the bishops that bitterness remained. He continued, *"When I gained my victories over my enemies, I thought nothing remained for me but to give thanks unto God and to rejoice with those who have been delivered by me. But when I learned, contrary to all expectations, that there were divisions among you, then I solemnly considered them, and praying that these discords might also be healed with my assistance, I summoned you here without delay. I rejoice to see you here, yet I should be more pleased to see unity and affection among you. I entreat you, therefore, beloved ministers of God, to remove the causes of dissension among you and to establish peace."*[180]

As we can see, there was now no way of mistaking the threat behind the words, and as though, the following day, to make his threat more clear, the emperor summoned one of his attendants and silently produced the parchment rolls and letters containing complaints and petitions that the bishops had privately sent him. A brazier was set up. The emperor tossed the petitions into the flames. While they were still burning, he explained that all these petitions would appear again on the day of judgment, and then the great Judge of all things would pass judgment on them: for himself he was content to listen to the public deliberations of the bishops and had not even read these bitter messages sent to him. By this he implied that most of the petitions from the bishops had been aimed at one another, and rather than put many on trial he had given a common amnesty[181].

---

180) Socratis Scolasticus, *Cit.*, II
181) D.Dudley, *History of the First council of Nice: A World's Christian Convention A.D. 325 With a Life of Constantine*, A & B Book Dist Inc, 2002, pp.71ff

So, finally, the theological discussion was ready to start.

At the beginning of the discussion the positions of the council fathers were basically three: briefly remembering them, Alexander and his followers (now known as "Homoousians"[182]) believed that the Son was of the same substance as the Father, co-eternal with him. The Arians believed that they were different and that the Son, though he may be the most perfect of creations, was only a creation. A third group (now known as "Homoiousians"[183]) tried to make a compromise position, saying that the Father and the Son were of similar substance.

As soon as the conference opened, the Arians and the anti-Arians were at one another's throats. Denunciation and angry accusation flew across the hall. Everyone was suddenly arguing. There was a wild waving of arms. *"It was like a battle in the dark"* the historian Socrates said later. *"Hardly anyone seemed to know the grounds on which they calumniated one another."*[184]

Constantine had invited Arius to be present and listened earnestly when Arius explained the nature of his beliefs, so he was not particularly surprised when Arius burst out into a long, sustained chant, having set his beliefs to music. These chants and songs were sung by the people, and Arius may have thought the emperor would listen more keenly to chanting than to a disquisition on the faith:

"The uncreated God has made the Son. A beginning of things created,
And by adoption has God made the Son Into an advancement of himself.
Yet the Son's substance is Removed from the substance of the Father: The
Son is not equal to the Father, nor does he share the same substance.
God is the all-wise Father, And the Son is the teacher of his mysteries.

---

182) From the Greek ομού meaning same and ουσία meaning essence or being

183) From the Greek όμοιος meaning similar and ουσία meaning essence or being

184) Socrates Scholasticus, *Cit.*, II

The members of the Holy Trinity Share unequal glories."[185]
The anti-Arian bishops were appalled, closed their eyes, and put their hands over their ears. It was as though, in the middle of a critical debate on the future of the world, someone interrupted with nonsense rhymes or a series of perplexing and meaningless mathematical equations. Yet the heart of the Arian mystery was in these rhymes sung to a music employed by the Alexandrian dance bands. Arius, gaunt, white-faced, his stringy hair reaching to his shoulders, could repulse any theological argument by simply chanting one of these songs.[186]

Athanasius (or perhaps some other father[187]) answered with a close-knit argument: there was consternation, for they seemed to be talking in different languages about different things, like two men from different worlds or different universes.

Probably Athanasius was standing just behind Pope Alexander and, therefore, very close to the emperor. We know that he attracted the emperor's attention[188], but it was not Athanasius who resolved the issue. It seems to have been Hosius who announced that the simplest way of reaching agreement would be to draw up a creed.

The first creed presented to the council was written by 18 (Sozomen states 22[189]) of the Arian bishops, led by Eusebius of Nicomedia and including some preeminent figures like the bishops Theognis of Nicea and Maris of Chalcedon. Couched in scriptural language, this creed stated the Arian position so offensively that when some of the most shocking passages from his writings were read, they were almost universally seen as

---

185) *Ibidem*
186) M.M.Arnold, *Nicaea and the Nicene Council of AD 325*, Arno Publications, 1987, p.36
187) Reports are not very clear and different fathers are mentioned by Eusebius, Athanasius and Socrates
188) Sozomen, *Cit.*, according to Carroll, *Cit.*, Chap.11
189) *Ibidem*

blasphemous and a big bedlam broke loose[190].

At this point, Eusebius of Caesarea, one of the paladins of the "via media", suggested a creed that he had first heard as a child and that was used in his own diocese at Caesarea in Palestine, as a form of reconciliation. It was an astonishingly beautiful creed that was for a long time thought to form the basis of the finally adopted creed, even if now most scholars think that nowadays creed is derived from the baptismal creed of Jerusalem, as Hans Lietzmann[191] proposed or from the Apostle's creed[192].

Eusebius was careful to say he advanced this creed only because he believed divine things cannot be fully expressed in human language: it was not perfect, but it was as close to perfection as he ever hoped to reach. This creed read:

"We believe in one only God, Father Almighty, Creator of things visible and invisible; and in the Lord Jesus Christ, for he is the Word of God, God of God, Light of Light, life of life, his only Son, the first-born of all creatures, begotten of the Father before all time, by whom also everything was created, who became flesh for our redemption, who lived and suffered amongst men, rose again the third day, returned to the Father, and will come again one day in his glory to judge the quick and the dead. We believe also in the Holy Ghost. We believe that each of these three is and subsists; the Father truly as Father, the Son truly as Son, the Holy Ghost truly as Holy Ghost; as our Lord also said, when he sent his disciples to preach: Go and teach all nations, and baptize them in the name of the Father, and of the Son, and of the Holy Ghost."[193]

This creed was immediately accepted by the emperor, and also the Arians, seeing in it nothing that specifically destroyed their position, would have accepted it. But their opponents, first of

---

190) *Ibidem*
191) H.Lietzman, *The Founding of the Church Universal - A History of the Early Church*, II, pp.163ff
192) E.Missing Sewell, *History of the Early Church from the First Preaching of the Gospel to the Council of Nicea*, D. Appleton and Company, 1884, p. 272
193) Reported by Eusebius in a letter to his Congregation

all bishop Alexander, objected that this creed failed in any way to resolve the conflict: it was necessary to state the creed in such a way that the Arians would be forced to deny their essential tenets[194].

Alexander discussed the matter with Hosius. Constantine, understanding the will of the majority and turning against the Arians he had previously favored, suggested that Christ should be defined as homoousios, one in essence with the Father, and this definition should be included in the creed[195].

The orthodox bishops were gaining more and more strength and unity and finally a new creed, formed by patching together the old creed and a new, more vigorous statement of the anti-Arian position, was announced by Hosius on the June 19th. It read:

"We believe in one God the Father Almighty, Maker of all things visible and invisible; and in one Lord Jesus Christ, the only begotten of the Father, that is, of the substance ["ek tes ousias"] *of the Father, God of God, light of light, true God of true God, begotten not made, of the same substance with the Father* ["homoousion to patri"], *through whom all things were made both in heaven and on earth; who for us men and our salvation descended, was incarnate, and was made man, suffered and rose again the third day, ascended into heaven and cometh to judge the living and the dead. And in the Holy Ghost. Those who say: There was a time when He was not, and He was not before He was begotten; and that He was made our of nothing* ["ex ouk onton"]; *or who maintain that He is of another hypostasis or another substance* [than the Father], *or that the Son of God is created, or mutable, or subject to change,* [them] *the Catholic Church anathematizes."*[196]

In this form, the Nicene creed left much to be desired. It was tortured, blunt-edged, without poetry or rhythm, and without

---

194) E.Missing Sewell, *Cit.*, pp.275ff
195) D.Dudley, *Cit.*, p.91
196) Eusebius of Cesarea, *Historia Ecclesiastica*, III

the nobility of the creed of the church of Palestine. But many words that gave a living significance to the original creed (*"the Word of God"*, *"the Firstborn of every creature"*, *"begotten of the Father before all worlds"*), were in fact deliberately omitted to show that the triumphant Alexandrians would allow no compromise, no loophole for the Arians and were bent on avoiding all misunderstanding.

For the same reason, other fundamental elements were added:
1. Jesus Christ is described as *"God from God, Light from Light, true God from true God"*, confirming his divinity. When all light sources were natural, the essence of light was considered to be identical, regardless of its form;
2. Jesus Christ is said to be *"begotten, not made"* asserting his co-eternalness with God, and confirming it by stating his role in the creation;
3. Finally, he is said to be *"from the substance of the Father"*, in direct opposition to Arianism[197].

Thus, instead of a baptismal creed acceptable to both the "homoousian" and Arian parties, as proposed by Eusebius, the council promulgated one which was unambiguous in the aspects touching upon the points of contention between these two positions, and one which was incompatible with the beliefs of Arians[198].

So, why did this become the official document of the council, with just a few objections? To understand this we must remember that Bishop Hosius of Cordova, one of the firm homoousians, and, according to Athanasius[199], the actual redactor of the final creed, was a very powerful man: at the time

---

197) Some ascribe the term "Consubstantial", (*"of the same substance"* of the Father), to Constantine who, on this particular point, may have chosen to exercise his authority. See: L.C. Jackson, *Cit.*, p.281

198) W.P. Loewe, *The College Student's Introduction to Christology*, Michael Glazier Books, 1996, p.97

199) Athanasius, *The Incarnation of the Word of God*, I

of the council, he was the confidant of the emperor in all Church matters and stood at the head of the lists of bishops. Moreover, great leaders such as Eustathius of Antioch, Alexander of Alexandria, Athanasius and Marcellus of Ancyra, all immediately adhered to the homoousian position of this new creed. In spite of his sympathy for Arius, Eusebius of Caesarea adhered to the decisions of the council too, accepting its final formulation. The initial number of bishops supporting Arius was already at the beginning quite small but, after a month of discussion and possibly of pressures[200], on June 19th, there were only two left: Theonas of Marmarica in Libya, and Secundus of Ptolemais. Even Maris of Chalcedon, who initially supported Arianism, agreed to the new creed and, similarly, Eusebius of Nicomedia (for whom to disagree with the imperial position would have been particularly difficult, being the bishop of the imperial seat[201]) and Theognis of Nicea also agreed, although expressing their doubts about some statements[202].

The emperor, now, played a decisive card, carrying out his earlier statement: everybody who refuses to endorse the creed would be exiled. Arius, Theonas, and Secundus anyway refused to adhere to the creed, and were thus exiled, in addition to being excommunicated. The works of Arius were ordered to be confiscated and consigned to the flames[203], although there is no evidence that this occurred. Even if the controversy continued in various parts of the empire, this put an end to the Christological discussion of the council.

After the settlement of the most important topic, the council fathers passed to the discussion of other much less problematic matters such as the question of the date of the Christian

---

200) H.A. Drake, *Constantine and the Bishops: The Politics of Intolerance*, Cit., p. 107
201) *Ibidem*, p. 109
202) Socrates Scholasticus, *Cit.*, I, 8
203) Socrates Scholasticus, *Cit.*, I, 9

Passover (Easter), the suppression of the Meletian schism and problems related to the clergy life-style. In the meanwhile, they had already started to write the final documents of the council, containing the new church laws, called canons (that is, unchanging rules of discipline), resulting from the synod and the *Synodal Letter*, addressed in particular to the Church of Alexandria (where the whole Arian problem had started) but open to the whole Christianity containing the news related to the major items of discussion (which we will analyze focusing on the documents of the council).

The council came to an end on July 25th with a solemn banquet ordered by the emperor for his twentieth anniversary. The bishops had deliberated for nearly seven weeks, debating on 84 subjects[204], and now, exhausted, they prepared to make their way homeward. The last speeches had been made.

There remained only the ceremonial leave-taking at the banquet, with the emperor sitting at a table in the midst of them.

Constantine, as usual stiff with purple, gold, and precious stones, was in good humor. After his valedictory address, in which he again informed his hearers how averse he was to dogmatic controversy, and how he wanted the Church to live in harmony and peace, he complimented Athanasius, gave presents to the bishops he favored, and at one point, he summoned the unregenerate Bishop Acesius, who possessed a singular regard for the Novatian heresy, which held that only God had the power to pardon sins and that anyone who committed sin after baptism had to be permanently refused Communion. Constantine reminded Acesius that the doctrine of the Church was now finally established. Acesius made a long speech in defense of his puritan interpretation of the Scriptures. Constantine guffawed, "*Ho, ho, Acesius! Now plant a ladder and*

---

204) According to the Arabic version of the Canon found in the XVI century

climb up to heaven by yourself?'. Sometime later, Constantine summoned the saintly Bishop Paphnutius and kissed the empty socket, and pressed his legs and arms to the paralyzed limbs, and he was especially gentle to all the other bishops who had suffered under the persecutions[205].

After he promised that, in a circular letter, he would have announced the accomplished unity of practice by the whole Church (which he actually did), the bishops went out through a line of imperial bodyguards with bared swords: the council was finally over.

---

205) Sozomen, *Cit.*, II

Dr. Lawrence M.F. Sudbury – **Nicea: what it was, what it was not**

III

THE DOCUMENTS

Dr. Lawrence M.F. Sudbury – **Nicea: what it was, what it was not**

III.1) THE FINAL DOCUMENTS

An element we must always keep in our mind is that any account used to build any possible report or history of the council of Nicea is, finally, as already noted, subjective. All the writers, both the ones concretely participating to the sessions of the synod and the ones recollecting pieces of information (basically second-hand pieces of information) in the following years and centuries were somehow, with different roles, involved in a theological, historical and political process of progressive definition of the Christian Church and, therefore, were inevitably partisan in their reports.

We have, anyway, some elements we can consider, even if only partly, more objective as sources of the decisions of Nicea: the final documents of the council. Actually, also in this case, it must be remembered that only incomplete records of this documents still exist: what we actually have is the creed and the disciplinary action against the Arians we already spoke about, the disciplinary canons, a letter to the Alexandrian church and a list of the bishops attending the meeting (a list which varies from language to language). Obviously we can speak about only a partial objectivity, as all these documents arrived to us through reports more or less of the same writers thanks to whom we inherited the accounts about the council development, but, at least, the variety of the attestations and the uniformity of the textual sources can grant us to read something very similar to what was produced by the bishops in Nicea.

Among these documents, the ones being most interesting to us, but for the already analyzed creed, are the *Synodal Letter* and the *Canon*. In this part we will only see the texts and their history, delaying any comment to the following chapters of this section.

The *Synodal Letter* appears for the first time in our documents in a letter of Athanasius[206] which is a masterpiece of ideological manipulation, through which the Nicene bishops tried to present in a triumphal way an "orthodox victory", whose central theme is the Arian "discourse", where the defeated party recognized that they were the enemies of Christ. The text, later reported by Gelasius[207], Socrates Scholasticus[208] and Theodoretus[209], is so similar (practically identical) in all versions that it is hard to understand whether all subsequent copies take from Athanasius or if there is a common base for all writings (including Athanasius), perhaps being the original writing of the council fathers.

The text is the following:

"To the Church of Alexandria, by the grace of God, holy and great; and to our well-beloved brethren, the orthodox clergy and laity throughout Egypt, and Pentapolis, and Lybia, and every nation under heaven, the holy and great synod, the bishops assembled at Nicea, wish health in the Lord.

Forasmuch as the great and holy Synod, which was assembled at Niece through the grace of Christ and our most religious Sovereign Constantine, who brought us together from our several provinces and cities, has considered matters which concern the faith of the Church, it seemed to us to be necessary that certain things should be communicated from us to you in writing, so that you might have the means of knowing what has been mooted and investigated, and also what has been decreed and confirmed.

First of all, then, in the presence of our most religious Sovereign Constantine, investigation was made of matters concerning the impiety and transgression of Arius and his adherents; and it was unanimously decreed that he and his impious opinion should be anathematized, together with the blasphemous words and speculations in which he indulged, blaspheming the Son of God, and saying that he is from things that are not, and that before he was begotten he was not, and that there was a time when he was not, and

---

206) Athanasius, *Epistula XLVII*
207) Gelasius, *Historia Concilii Nicæni*, II. 33
208) Socrates Scolasticus, *Cit.*, I. 6
209) Theodoretus, *Historia Ecclesiae*, I.9

that the Son of God is by his free will capable of vice and virtue; saying also that he is a creature. All these things the holy Synod has anathematized, not even enduring to hear his impious doctrine and madness and blasphemous words. And of the charges against him and of the results they had, ye have either already heard or will hear the particulars, lest we should seem to be oppressing a man who has in fact received a fitting recompense for his own sin. So far indeed has his impiety prevailed, that he has even destroyed Theonas of Marmorica and Secundes of Ptolemais; for they also have received the same sentence as the rest.

But when the grace of God had delivered Egypt from that heresy and blasphemy, and from the persons who have dared to make disturbance and division among a people heretofore at peace, there remained the matter of the insolence of Meletius and those who have been ordained by him; and concerning this part of our work we now, beloved brethren, proceed to inform you of the decrees of the Synod. The Synod, then, being disposed to deal gently with Meletius (for in strict justice he deserved no leniency), decreed that he should remain in his own city, but have no authority either to ordain, or to administer affairs, or to make appointments; and that he should not appear in the country or in any other city for this purpose, but should enjoy the bare title of his rank; but that those who have been placed by him, after they have been confirmed by a more sacred laying on of hands, shall on these conditions be admitted to communion: that they shall both have their rank and the right to officiate, but that they shall be altogether the inferiors of all those who are enrolled in any church or parish, and have been appointed by our most honourable colleague Alexander. So that these men are to have no authority to make appointments of persons who may be pleasing to them, nor to suggest names, nor to do anything whatever, without the consent of the bishops of the Catholic and Apostolic Church, who are serving under our most holy colleague Alexander; while those who, by the grace of God and through your prayers, have been found in no schism, but on the contrary are without spot in the Catholic and Apostolic Church, are to have authority to make appointments and nominations of worthy persons among the clergy, and in short to do all things according to the law and ordinance of the Church. But, if it happen that any of the clergy who are now in the Church should die, then those who have been lately received are to succeed to the office of the deceased; always provided that they shall appear to be worthy, and that the people elect them, and that the bishop of Alexandria shall concur in the election and ratify it. This concession has been made to all the rest; but, on account of his disorderly conduct from the first, and the rashness and precipitation of his character, the same decree was not p. 54 made concerning Meletius himself, but that, inasmuch as he is a man capable of committing again the same disorders, no authority nor privilege should be conceded to him.

These are the particulars, which are of special interest to Egypt and to the most holy Church of Alexandria; but if in the presence of our most honored lord, our colleague and brother Alexander, anything else has been enacted by canon or other decree, he will himself convey it to you in greater detail, he having been both a guide and fellow-worker in what has been done.

We further proclaim to you the good news of the agreement concerning the holy Easter, that this particular also has through your prayers been rightly settled; so that all our brethren in the East who formerly followed the custom of the Jews are henceforth to celebrate the said most sacred feast of Easter at the same time with the Romans and yourselves and all those who have observed Easter from the beginning.

Wherefore, rejoicing in these wholesome results, and in our common peace and harmony, and in the cutting off of every heresy, receive ye with the greater honor and with increased love, our colleague your Bishop Alexander, who has gladdened us by his presence, and who at so great an age has undergone so great fatigue that peace might be established among you and all of us. Pray ye also for us all, that the things which have been deemed advisable may stand fast; for they have been done, as we believe, to the well-pleasing of Almighty God and of his only Begotten Son, our Lord Jesus Christ, and of the Holy Ghost, to whom be glory for ever. Amen."[210]

In relation to the canons, things seem to be less easy, mainly in

---

210) Translation from Athanasius, *Epistula XLVII*

terms of philology.

First of all, let's remember what a canon is. "Κανον", as an ecclesiastical term, has a very interesting history[211]. The original sense, "a straight rod" or "line," determines all its religious applications, which begin with St. Paul's use of it for a prescribed sphere of apostolic work[212] or a regulative principle of Christian life[213]. It represents the element of definiteness in Christianity and in the order of the Christian Church. Clement of Rome[214] and many others after him, used it for the measure of Christian attainment and when Basil spoke of *"the transmitted canon of true religion"*[215] the term became equivalent to the statement of a "regula fidei" Thus it was natural for Socrates to call the Nicene creed itself a "canon"[216]. Properly, anyway, in relation to the Nicene council, when we speak about "canon", we generally refer to a standing "canon of discipline" particularly targeted to the clergy and the members of the Church[217].

The real problem of the Nicene canon is not, anyway, the one of a definition, but the one of the sources and, in relation to this, the one of the possible missing canons in our heritage.

The trouble exists as we have a Latin letter purporting to have been written by Athanasius to Pope Marcus. This letter was found in the Benedictine edition of Athanasius's works[218] and contains the assertion that the council of Nicea at first adopted forty canons, which were in Greek, that it subsequently added

---

211) P. Westcott, *On the New Testament Canon*, MacMillan, 1855, p. 498 ff
212) 2 Cor. 10:13, 15
213) Gal. 6:16
214) Clement of Rome, *Epistle to the Corinthians*, VII
215) Basil, *Epistulae*, CCIV.6
216) Socrates Scholasticus, *Cit.*, II.27
217) J.T. Lienhard, *The Bible, the Church, and Authority: The Canon of the Christian Bible in History and Theology*, Michael Glazier Books, 1995, p.18
218) Ed. Patav. II. 599, rejected as spurious by some scholars

twenty Latin canons, and that afterwards the council reassembled and set forth seventy altogether. A tradition that something of this kind had taken place was, anyway. already prevalent in many parts of the East, and some collections did contain up to seventy canons.

Moreover, in the Vatican Library, in a manuscript bought from the Coptic Patriarch John, we find not only seventy, but eighty canons attributed to the council of Nicea. The manuscript is in Arabic, and was discovered by J. B. Romanus, S. J., who first translated into Latin a copy he had made of it, making its contents known in the latter half of the sixteenth century.

So, why does the tradition, set by Athanasius[219], reports only twenty canons?

The question still stands at these days.

Hefele[220] says, *"it is certain that the Orientals believed the council of Nicea to have promulgated more than twenty canons: the learned Anglican, Beveridge, has proved this, reproducing an ancient Arabic paraphrase of the canons of the first four Ecumenical Councils. According to this Arabic paraphrase, found in a manuscript. in the Bodleian Library, the council of Nicea must have put forth three books of canons [...] The Arabic paraphrase of which we are speaking gives a paraphrase of all these canons, but Beveridge took only the part referring to the second book, that is to say, the paraphrase of the twenty genuine canons; for, according to his view, which was perfectly correct, it was only these twenty canons which were really the work of the council of Nicea, and all the others were falsely attributed to it."* Hefele goes on to prove that the canons he rejects must be of much later origin, some being laws of the times of Theodosius and Justinian.

This is surely possible, but, on the other hand, many others[221]

---

219) Athanasius, *Cit.*, II
220) K.J. Von Hefele, *A History of the Councils of the Church, from the Original Documents*, Vol. I., Reprint: Ams Pr Inc, 1975, pp. 355ff
221) In example K.Kirshenhousen, *Patristic Philology*, Haberdorff, 1983, passim and A.Reedson, *The post-Nicean Faith*, Spencer&Co., 1991, passim

have held that, if not all, at least many of the canons of the Arabic manuscript could have been truly composed by the council bishops.

Anybody can make his own mind having a look to the "Arabic canon" reported in "Appendix I", but any decision should keep into account the testimony of those Greek and Latin authors who lived about the time of the council and have given their opinion in relation to the number of the canons:

a. the first to be consulted among the Greek authors is the learned Theodoret, who lived about a century after the council of Nicea. He says, in his *History of the Church*: *"After the condemnation of the Arians, the bishops assembled once more, and decreed twenty canons on ecclesiastical discipline."*[222];

b. twenty years later, Gelasius, Bishop of Cyzicus, after much research into the most ancient documents, wrote a history of the Nicene council. Gelasius also expressly says that the council decreed twenty canons; and, what is more important, he gives the original text of these canons exactly in the same order and according to the same tenor which we find in many other sources[223];

c. Rufinus is more ancient than the previous two historians. He was born near the period when the council of Nicea was held, and about half a century later he wrote his celebrated *History of the Church*, in which he inserted a Latin translation of the Nicene canons. Rufinus also knew only of these twenty canons; but as he has divided the sixth and the eighth into two parts, he has given twenty-two canons, which are exactly the same as the twenty furnished by the other historians[224];

d. All the ancient collections of canons, either in Latin or Greek, composed in the IV, or quite certainly at least in the V

---

222) Theodoret, *Historia Ecclesiae*, I.7
223) Gelasius, *Syntagma*, II.34
224) Rufinus of Aquileia, *Historia Ecclesiastica*, XII

century, agree in giving only these twenty canons to Nicea. The most ancient of these collections were made in the Greek Church, and in the course of time a very great number of copies of them were written. Many of these copies have descended to us.

The Latin collections of the canons of the councils also give the same result (for example, the most ancient and the most remarkable of all, the *Prisca*[225], and that of Dionysius the Less[226], which was collected about A.D. 500).

f. Among the later Eastern witnesses we may further mention Photius, Zonaras and Balsamon. Photius, in his *Collection of the Canons*[227], and in his *Nomocanon*[228], as well as the two other writers in their commentaries upon the canons of the ancient councils, quote and know only twenty canons of Nicea, and always those which we possess.

For all these reasons we tend to agree with Hefele in considering all the other Canons as later additions. Therefore, on the basis of this conception, the canonical text should read as follows:

"*Canon 1*

If anyone in sickness has been subjected by physicians to a surgical operation, or if he has been castrated by barbarians, let him remain among the clergy; but, if any one in sound health has castrated himself, it behoves that such an one, if [already] *enrolled among the clergy, should cease [from his ministry], and that from henceforth no such person should be promoted. But, as it is evident that this is said of those who wilfully do the thing and presume to castrate themselves, so if any have been made eunuchs by barbarians, or by their masters, and should otherwise be found worthy, such men the Canon admits to the clergy.*

Canon 2

---

225) *Isidoriana, Versio Prisca*, I
226) Dionysius Exiguus, *Liber Canonum*, I
227) Photius Constantinopolitanus, *Collectionem Canonum*, I
228) Iohannes Scholasticus, *Nomocanon*, III

Forasmuch as, either from necessity, or through the urgency of individuals, many things have been done contrary to the Ecclesiastical canon, so that men just converted from heathenism to the faith, and who have been instructed but a little while, are straightway brought to the spiritual laver, and as soon as they have been baptized, are advanced to the episcopate or the presbyterate, it has seemed right to us that for the time to come no such thing shall be done. For to the catechumen himself there is need of time and of a longer trial after baptism. For the apostolical saying is clear, Not a novice; lest, being lifted up with pride, he fall into condemnation and the snare of the devil. But if, as time goes on, any sensual sin should be found out about the person, and he should be convicted by two or three witnesses, let him cease from the clerical office. And whoso shall transgress these [enactments] *will imperil his own clerical position, as a person who presumes to disobey the great Synod.*

<u>Canon 3</u>
The great Synod has stringently forbidden any bishop, presbyter, deacon, or any one of the clergy whatever, to have a subintroducta dwelling with him, except only a mother, or sister, or aunt, or such persons only as are beyond all suspicion.

<u>Canon 4</u>
It is by all means proper that a bishop should be appointed by all the bishops in the province; but should this be difficult, either on account of urgent necessity or because of distance, three at least should meet together, and the suffrages of the absent [bishops] *also being given and communicated in writing, then the ordination should take place. But in every province the ratification of what is done should be left to the Metropolitan.*

<u>Canon 5</u>
Concerning those, whether of the clergy or of the laity, who have been excommunicated in the several provinces, let the provision of the canon be observed by the bishops which provides that persons cast out by some be not readmitted by others. Nevertheless, inquiry should be made whether they have been excommunicated through captiousness, or contentiousness, or any such like ungracious disposition in the bishop. And, that this matter may

have due investigation, it is decreed that in every province synods shall be held twice a year, in order that when all the bishops of the province are assembled together, such questions may by them be thoroughly examined, that so those who have confessedly offended against their bishop, may be seen by all to be for just cause excommunicated, until it shall seem fit to a general meeting of the bishops to pronounce a milder sentence upon them. And let these synods be held, the one before Lent, (that the pure Gift may be offered to God after all bitterness has been put away), and let the second be held about autumn.

Canon 6
Let the ancient customs in Egypt, Libya and Pentapolis prevail, that the Bishop of Alexandria have jurisdiction in all these, since the like is customary for the Bishop of Rome also. Likewise in Antioch and the other provinces, let the Churches retain their privileges. And this is to be universally understood, that if any one be made bishop without the consent of the Metropolitan, the great Synod has declared that such a man ought not to be a bishop. If, however, two or three bishops shall from natural love of contradiction, oppose the common suffrage of the rest, it being reasonable and in accordance with the ecclesiastical law, then let the choice of the majority prevail.

Canon 7
Since custom and ancient tradition have prevailed that the Bishop of Ælia [i.e., Jerusalem] should be honoured, let him, saving its due dignity to the Metropolis, have the next place of honour.

Canon 8
Concerning those who call themselves Cathari, if they come over to the Catholic and Apostolic Church, the great and holy Synod decrees that they who are ordained shall continue as they are in the clergy. But it is before all things necessary that they should profess in writing that they will observe and follow the dogmas of the Catholic and Apostolic Church; in particular that they will communicate with persons who have been twice married, and with those who having lapsed in persecution have had a period [of penance] laid upon them, and a time [of restoration] fixed so that in all things they will follow the dogmas of the Catholic Church. Wheresoever,

then, whether in villages or in cities, all of the ordained are found to be of these only, let them remain in the clergy, and in the same rank in which they are found. But if they come over where there is a bishop or presbyter of the Catholic Church, it is manifest that the Bishop of the Church must have the bishop's dignity; and he who was named bishop by those who are called Cathari shall have the rank of presbyter, unless it shall seem fit to the Bishop to admit him to partake in the honour of the title. Or, if this should not be satisfactory, then shall the bishop provide for him a place as Chorepiscopus, or presbyter, in order that he may be evidently seen to be of the clergy, and that there may not be two bishops in the city.

Canon 9
If any presbyters have been advanced without examination, or if upon examination they have made confession of crime, and men acting in violation of the canon have laid hands upon them, notwithstanding their confession, such the canon does not admit; for the Catholic Church requires that [only] which is blameless.

Canon 10
If any who have lapsed have been ordained through the ignorance, or even with the previous knowledge of the ordainers, this shall not prejudice the canon of the Church; for when they are discovered they shall be deposed.

Canon 11
Concerning those who have fallen without compulsion, without the spoiling of their property, without danger or the like, as happened during the tyranny of Licinius, the Synod declares that, though they have deserved no clemency, they shall be dealt with mercifully. As many as were communicants, if they heartily repent, shall pass three years among the hearers; for seven years they shall be prostrators; and for two years they shall communicate with the people in prayers, but without oblation.

Canon 12
As many as were called by grace, and displayed the first zeal, having cast aside their military girdles, but afterwards returned, like dogs, to their own vomit, (so that some spent money and by means of gifts regained their military stations); let these, after they have passed the space of three years as hearers, be for ten years prostrators. But in all these cases it is necessary

to examine well into their purpose and what their repentance appears to be like. For as many as give evidence of their conversions by deeds, and not pretence, with fear, and tears, and perseverance, and good works, when they have fulfilled their appointed time as hearers, may properly communicate in prayers; and after that the bishop may determine yet more favourably concerning them. But those who take [the matter] with indifference, and who think the form of [not] entering the Church is sufficient for their conversion, must fulfill the whole time.

Canon 13
Concerning the departing, the ancient canonical law is still to be maintained, to wit, that, if any man be at the point of death, he must not be deprived of the last and most indispensable Viaticum. But, if any one should be restored to health again who has received the communion when his life was despaired of, let him remain among those who communicate in prayers only. But in general, and in the case of any dying person whatsoever asking to receive the Eucharist, let the Bishop, after examination made, give it him.

Canon 14
Concerning catechumens who have lapsed, the holy and great Synod has decreed that, after they have passed three years only as hearers, they shall pray with the catechumens.

Canon 15
On account of the great disturbance and discords that occur, it is decreed that the custom prevailing in certain places contrary to the Canon, must wholly be done away; so that neither bishop, presbyter, nor deacon shall pass from city to city. And if any one, after this decree of the holy and great Synod, shall attempt any such thing, or continue in any such course, his proceedings shall be utterly void, and he shall be restored to the Church for which he was ordained bishop or presbyter.

Canon 16
Neither presbyters, nor deacons, nor any others enrolled among the clergy, who, not having the fear of God before their eyes, nor regarding the ecclesiastical Canon, shall recklessly remove from their own church, ought by any means to be received by another church; but every constraint should be

applied to restore them to their own parishes; and, if they will not go, they must be excommunicated. And if anyone shall dare surreptitiously to carry off and in his own Church ordain a man belonging to another, without the consent of his own proper bishop, from whom although he was enrolled in the clergy list he has seceded, let the ordination be void.

Canon 17

Forasmuch as many enrolled among the Clergy, following covetousness and lust of gain, have forgotten the divine Scripture, which says, He has not given his money upon usury, and in lending money ask the hundredth of the sum [as monthly interest], the holy and great Synod thinks it just that if after this decree any one be found to receive usury, whether he accomplish it by secret transaction or otherwise, as by demanding the whole and one half, or by using any other contrivance whatever for filthy lucre's sake, he shall be deposed from the clergy and his name stricken from the list.

Canon 18

It has come to the knowledge of the holy and great Synod that, in some districts and cities, the deacons administer the Eucharist to the presbyters, whereas neither canon nor custom permits that they who have no right to offer should give the Body of Christ to them that do offer. And this also has been made known, that certain deacons now touch the Eucharist even before the bishops. Let all such practices be utterly done away, and let the deacons remain within their own bounds, knowing that they are the ministers of the bishop and the inferiors of the presbyters. Let them receive the Eucharist according to their order, after the presbyters, and let either the bishop or the presbyter administer to them. Furthermore, let not the deacons sit among the presbyters, for that is contrary to canon and order. And if, after this decree, any one shall refuse to obey, let him be deposed from the diaconate.

Canon 19

Concerning the Paulianists who have flown for refuge to the Catholic Church, it has been decreed that they must by all means be rebaptized; and if any of them who in past time have been numbered among their clergy should be found blameless and without reproach, let them be rebaptized and *ordained by the Bishop of the Catholic Church; but if the examination should discover them to be unfit, they ought to be deposed. Likewise in the case of their deaconesses, and generally in the case of those who have been enrolled among their clergy, let the same form be observed. And we mean by deaconesses such as have assumed the habit, but who, since they have no imposition of hands, are to be numbered only among the laity.*

<u>Canon 20</u>

Forasmuch as there are certain persons who kneel on the Lord's Day and in the days of Pentecost, therefore, to the intent that all things may be uniformly observed everywhere (in every parish), it seems good to the holy Synod that prayer be made to God standing."[229]

Obviously, in themselves, both the *Synodal Letter* and the *Canons* give us only a sort of snapshot of the solutions given by the Nicene fathers to some problems of the Church, but to understand these problems we need to analyze them more in depth.

---

229) Text in: A.Roberts, J.Donaldson, P.Schaff, H.Wace, *Nicene and Post-Nicene Fathers*, Ser.II, Vol. XIV, Hendrickson Publishers, 1994, passim

III.2) THE SYNODAL LETTER

As mentioned, the *Synodal Letter* is, at the same time, an addressed letter (*"To the Church of Alexandria [...]; and to our well-beloved brethren, the orthodox clergy and laity throughout Egypt, and Pentapolis, and Lybia [...]"*) and an ecumenical letter *("and* [to] *every nation under heaven ...").* The need for an addressed letter was quite obvious, as Alexandria and the nearby areas had been the springs of the principal controversies treated during the council, and we have a great echo of the need to re-establish a correct asset of the church in those dioceses in the strong emphasis given in various passages to the figure of Alexander, the legitimate and "orthodox" patriarch of the town. But, on the other hand, the troubles of the North-African church had had consequences spreading in all directions and mining the unity of the Christian Church mainly in the near-East area. From these, the need for the council bishops to diffuse the news about a supposed re-established unity and to give to all churches information about the decisions concerning the three most important matters discussed in the Synod: the Arian heresy, the Melitian heresy and the date of Easter.

But for noting, in the *Letter*, a rather evident (and, somehow, perfectly understandable in the light of the must to show a community of intent by the church leaders) contradiction between the statement of a unanimous decision of condemnation of Arianism and, a few lines below, the report of the dissent by Theonas of Marmorica and Secundes of Ptolemais, we have already been speaking about the Arian dispute enough not to come back over it again. Before analyzing the second "heresy" the council had to face, the Melitian one, it is interesting to concentrate our attention as first on the discussion related to the date of Easter.

To realize the need for a council decision about a thing many of us possibly never thought about, we must understand that, although probably few Christians today have ever heard of the word "Quartodeciman" (refering to the 14th day of the month), to those Christians who lived in the last half of the second century A.D., this word meant a real problem, so much that a great controversy, precisely known as "Quartodecimam controversy" arose between the churches of the East and those of the West about it.

The controversy involved three events: the contrast between Polycarp, the bishop of Smyrna, and Anicetus, the bishop of Rome, that occurred around A.D. 155; the more heated conflict between Polycrates, the bishop of Ephesus, and Victor, the bishop of Rome, that broke out around A.D. 195; and , obviously, the decree of Constantine following the Nicene council in A.D. 325.

Scholars disagree about the details of the controversy.

Briefly summarizing the main terms of the question[230], it seems that, in the II century, some Christian authorities wondered if Christianity should follow the Jews in the celebration of Easter. Two such authorities were Polycarp and Anicetus, the Bishop of Rome. The problem, practically, involved the time for celebrating the Eucharist (the Lord's Supper).

Polycarp had been ordained, according to the early Christian scholar Irenaeus, by the apostles themselves[231]. Since Irenaeus as a youth had heard Polycarp speaking about his conversations with the apostle John[232], this is a quite powerful evidence that the opinions of Polycarp could very well tally with those which were once expressed by John. Certainly, Polycarp had a deep respect for John and his authority and it could be said, with a great deal of confidence, that he was the successor of John as leader of the Christian church in the region of Asia Minor.

---

230) On the base of E.L. Martin, *The original Bible restored*, ASK Publications, 1984, passim
231) Eusebius of Caesarea, *Historia Ecclesiastica*, IV.14
232) *Ibidem*, V.20

The difficulty in relation to the "Quartodeciman Controversy" came to prominence in A.D. 154 when Polycarp made a journey to Rome in order to talk with Anicetus (the Bishop of the city) about this matter. The trouble concerned the time for completing a short fast period before the celebration of the Eucharist and a few other minor questions of difference between the churches of Asia Minor and those under the leadership of the Roman church. Polycarp stated most emphatically that he, and the other Bishops of Asia Minor, had been taught by the apostle John to observe the time of the Eucharist on the fourteenth day of the first Jewish month, on the day before the Passover of the Jews. This meant that the time for celebration could fall out to any day of the week. The Romans, however, had started, about A.D. 140, to keep the Eucharist on a Sunday following the Passover week.

Polycarp was unable to persuade the Bishop of Rome to abandon this new method of observation adopted by the Romans, even though he evoked the authority of John for his case. In fact, Anicetus had some definite reasons for not accepting the Jewish manner of calculating their calendar, in particular the fact that the Jews had recently made a change in the way they began their months and years. What had the Jews done to their calendar about the year A.D. 142? To understand it, we have to go back a little in time.

In A.D. 70 the city of Jerusalem had been destroyed and the Jews were no longer able to maintain their Sanhedrin (their Supreme Religious Court) at Jerusalem. It was this court that was in charge of all calendar matters. After A.D. 70, the Sanhedrin moved to a coastal city called Jamnia (not too far from modern Tel Aviv). While at this new headquarters Jewish religious authorities continued to send out their authoritative announcements to the various Jewish communities scattered around the world regarding the times for the beginnings of the sacred years and months.

Unfortunately in A.D. 132, the Jews went to war once again with the Romans. This time the consequences were even more disastrous for the Jewish religious authorities. The emperor Hadrian again destroyed Jerusalem and forbade any Sanhedrin from operating at Jamnia. This caused chaos in the Jewish religious world regarding the proclamation of the Jewish calendar dates for the celebration of the Mosaic festivals. This is where the problem concerning the Jewish calendar had its real beginning (and note that this was about 35 years after the death of the apostle John).

The Jewish authorities moved the Sanhedrin to a small town in Galilee called Usha. This was too far from Jerusalem to officially observe the moon to determine accurate times for calendar dates. So they devised a new type of calendar, very similar to the one that existed before, but based on calculation rather than observation. It was because the Jews accepted this different calendar that some Christians expressed displeasure. There were reasons why the alterations were objected to, and the objections even seemed logical on the surface. Let us look at the problem a little closer.

The Jewish year was a Lunar-Solar one. The normal Lunar Year is about 11 days shorter than the Solar and about every three years an extra (thirteenth) Lunar month had to be added to the calendar in order to keep it abreast with Solar time. In a period of 19 years, there were seven extra months added to the calendar in order to maintain the Jewish festivals in their proper seasons of the Solar Year. This was not done haphazardly. In fact, it required the official body of Jewish elders in Jerusalem (when the Sanhedrin was there) and then at Jamnia to accomplish this task. The Jewish community throughout the world was then informed, usually a year or so in advance, when the proper years and months could begin.

After the disastrous war of A.D. 132 to A.D. 135, when the Sanhedrin located at Jamnia was prevented from functioning, the Jews throughout the world were denied any official sanction for the beginnings of their years and months. Confusion resulted over the Jewish calendar: it meant that no "Leap Months" (the thirteenth months) were being utilized. Progressively, the Jewish festivals began to be celebrated eleven days earlier each year. Without the addition of the "Leap Months," by A.D. 142, the Passover was beginning to be observed as early as January[233]: this was an intolerable situation and something had to be done about it.

A solution was accomplished by the establishment of the new Sanhedrin at Usha. Thanks to this new institution, the Jews were once again provided with official pronouncements concerning the times of the beginnings of their years and months but, as the emperor Hadrian had forbidden any Jew from approaching the city of Jerusalem, the new calendar, as said, had to be based only on calculations. This presented a problem to Christians because the new calendar had one feature about it which was offensive to many of them. In fact, in the 17th year of the new Jewish calendar cycle the Passover happened to occur two days before the Vernal Equinox (the time for the beginning of Spring). This was contrary to all tradition of earlier times as in the past it had become a cardinal rule that Passover had to be celebrated after the start of Spring: Anatolius, an early Christian scholar, called attention to the fact that all previous Jewish authorities vouched that in the time of Christ the Passover was always held after the Vernal Equinox. He said: *"This may be learned from what is said by Philo, Josephus, and Musaeus; and not only by them, but also by those yet more ancient, the two Agathobuli, surnamed 'Masters,' and the famous Aristobulus, who was chosen by among the seventy interpreters for the sacred and divine Hebrew Scriptures. [...] All these writers, explaining questions in regard to the*

---

233) L.Finkelstein, *Akiba: Scholar, Saint and Martyr*, Jewish Publication Society, 1962, pp. 236–239, 274

Exodus, say that all alike should sacrifice the passover offerings after the Vernal Equinox in the first month."[234]

And, in the very year that Polycarp went to Rome to inform Anicetus that the Eucharist should be celebrated according to the calendar of the Jews, that year was the 17th of the Jewish Metonic cycle. Anicetus couldn't accept his ideas as it placed the time of Passover back into the winter season: as a matter of fact, when the Jewish calendar began to be in disarray at the end of the Jewish-Roman War, many Christian authorities took it upon themselves to calculate their own Full Moon for the Eucharist ceremonies. And some, notably those at Rome, simply abandoned an association of the Eucharist with the Full Moon and decided to observe it on a Sunday (the day of Christ's resurrection) after the Full Moon of Spring had occurred.

The Roman argument was simple: why should the Christians let the Jews tell them when the year had to begin and when they ought to celebrate their Eucharist, which up to that time had normally been observed on Nisan 14, the day before the Jewish Passover? After all, the Christians had as good astronomers as the Jews (so it was believed) and they did not feel it was necessary to follow a "new-fangled" calendar which placed the Passover of the Jews two days before the start of Spring.

Most Christians in Egypt, Rome and Carthage simply gave up on the ability of the Jews to make a proper calendar so they abandoned any attempt to celebrate the Lord's Supper in conformity to the new calculated Jewish calendar. Polycarp, however, and most of the Christians who lived in Asia Minor felt it better to remain with the Jewish calendar determinations. That's why, Polycarp made his journey to Rome to discuss the matter with Anicetus on friendly terms.

As the two didn't find an agreement, they simply went on observing their own respective Eucharists and parted in an

---

234) Eusebius of Caesarea, *Cit.*, VII. 32:14–19

amicable manner. This shows that there were no other major doctrinal differences between the two church communities in A.D. 154. But it also does indicate that the opinions which came from those who followed directly in the footsteps of the apostle John in Asia Minor had no influence upon the clerics at Rome.

The parting of Polycarp and Anicetus in a friendly way was not the end of the story. About A.D. 190 her controversy came up over this same matter. This time, Victor, the Bishop of Rome, was not at all pleased with the people in Asia Minor, in particular with the Ephesian community led by the bishop Polycrates, who continued to follow the disciples of John. He brazenly excommunicated those who looked to this Eastern area as the center of Christian authority. Irenaeus, who had been a personal disciple of Polycarp (and was himself born in Asia Minor), while siding with the Roman way of calculating the time for the Eucharist, rebuked the Bishop of Rome for such a unilateral decision[235], but, again, it must be recognized that there is no hint that there were other major doctrinal differences between the two church regions[236]: when one surveys the letters of Clement, Ignatius, Polycarp and Justin (the top orthodox authorities of the II century), it seems that as far as basic doctrine was concerned, the churches around Ephesus would have been little different from those in Rome, except just in the matter of celebrating the Eucharist.

What we do find, on the other hand, is a distinct desire for some Bishops to exercise political and administrative power over others. Irenaeus considered this wrong and this is why he felt compelled to admonish Victor of Rome not to be so rash in his dealings with the churches of Asia Minor where John's disciples remained.

Nevertheless, Rome slowly began to exercise a position of

---

235) Eusebius of Caesarea, *Cit.*, V.24
236) *Ibidem*, IV.22

leadership among most Christian congregations. It was Cyprian the Bishop of Carthage, about A.D.250, who finally stated that Rome had inherited the Petrine authority of primacy, but even with this doctrine beginning to be used, Cyprian did not think this gave supreme authority to Rome in all doctrinal and administrative matters[237]. It was not until the council of Chalcedon in A.D. 451 that the "Petrine theory" of supremacy for the Roman Bishop was finally made "official" in the empire, and that is when Christ's reference of the "keys" being given to Peter was dogmatically introduced to prove that leadership[238].

As the matter was fundamentally only political and not theological and as, on the other hand, always on the political point of view, the unity of Christianity had to be considered much more important than a mere disquisition about a festivity date (which, as said, was somehow mining this unity), we can understand the reason for which it was quite easy for the council fathers in Nicea to find an agreement in a short time.

Moreover, once again the presence of Constantine at the Synod was fundamental in the resolution of this contrast. Theodoret recorded the Emperor as saying: *"It was, in the first place, declared improper to follow the custom of the Jews in the celebration of this holy festival, because, their hands having been stained with crime, the minds of these wretched men are necessarily blinded. [...] Let us, then, have nothing in common with the Jews, who are our adversaries. [...] avoiding all contact with that evil way. [...] who, after having compassed the death of the Lord, being out of their minds, are guided not by sound reason, but by an*

---

237) H.Newell Bate, *Catholic and Apostolic: collected papers of Cuthbert Hamilton Turner*, Mowbray 1931, p. 228. In fact, Cyprian even disputed with the Roman Bishop on numerous issues and quoted the statement of Christ (John 20:21ff) that "all the apostles" had been given a type of equal authority (Cyprian, *The Treatises of Cyprian*, I.4)

238) F.F. Bruce, *The Spreading Flame: The Rise and Progress of Christianity, from its first beginnings to the conversion of the English*, Eerdmans Publishing Co., 1979, p. 341

unrestrained passion, wherever their innate madness carries them. [...] a people so utterly depraved. [...] Therefore, this irregularity must be corrected, in order that we may no more have any thing in common with those parricides and the murderers of our Lord. [...] no single point in common with the perjury of the Jews."[239] Actually, Constantine was giving voice to a feeling of anti-Judaism (quite clear in the less and less veiled accusations of "deicide" against the Jews by many church fathers of the period) already spreading in the body of Christianity in the IV century[240] but, surely, as always during the council, he was also working for his own side, creating a distance between his new allies and a population who, all along its history, had showed to be at least unruly to the Roman domination and never wholly accepting the imperial authority[241]. And, as usual, his words didn't fall unheard: not only it was determined that what we today call our Easter celebrations had to replace any type of ceremony which might resemble the Jewish Passover, but so determined were Christians by this time to avoid any connection with Jewish calculations that, if by chance Easter would ever occur on the day of the Jewish Passover, Easter itself would be celebrated on a Sunday one week later.

If the solution to the "Quartodecimam controversy" was mainly due to political reasons, things were not so different in relation to another question which, once again was to be considered more political then theological[242], the one related to the "Meletian Schism".

---

239) Theodoret, *Cit.*, I.8
240) W.Harrelson, R.M. Falk, *Jews and Christians: A Troubled Family*, Abingdon Press 1990, pp.94ff
241) Let's not forget that the last mass riot in Judea, the so-called "Sephoris Revolt", took place only 26 years after the council (V.Matthews, *A Brief History of Ancient Israel*, Westminster John Knox Press 2002, pp.131-132)
242) So considered, in example, in F. and D.Radecki, *Tumultuous Times*, St. Joseph's Media, 2004, p. 356ff

The basis of this theoretically short-lasting schism are, practically, the same of the Donatism Constantine had already fought against: an extreme intransigence and rigorism by some members of the North African church. The leader of the heresy, from whom it takes its name, was Meletius, bishop of Lycopolis. The details of his life are not clear as we have conflicting accounts of it. Probably he was imprisoned for his Christianity during the persecution under Diocletian along with Peter of Alexandria and, apparently as early as during the persecution itself, Melitius began to refuse to receive in communion those Christians who had renounced their faith during the persecution and later repented of that choice.

Melitius' rigorous stance on this point stood in contrast to the earlier willingness of bishops to accept back into communion those who seemed to have truly repented (a pattern which was addressed during previous similar controversies, including those about the lapsed during the Decian persecution about 50 years earlier). Once free, Melitius took more and more distance from Peter and the other bishops, maintaining his extreme position and, as his see of Lycopolis stood next in rank to that of Alexandria, of which Peter was bishop (A.D. 300–311), Meletius took advantage of Peter's flight from persecution[243] to intrude into his and other dioceses, ordain priests, and assume the character of primate of Egypt. A protest against his conduct by four incarcerated Egyptian bishops, Hesychius, Pachomius, Theodore, and Phileas, urged that his act was uncalled-for and carried out without consulting them or Peter, involving a breach of the rule which forbade one bishop to intrude into the diocese of another. Meletius ignored the protest. The bishops were martyred, and Meletius went to Alexandria. He was received by the two elders, Isidore and the afterwards famous Arius, and, probably at their instigation, he excommunicated

---

243) Sozomen, *Cit.*, I.24

two visitors appointed by Peter and replaced them by others. The archbishop of Alexandria then wrote forbidding his flock to have fellowship with Meletius until these acts had been investigated. A synod of Egyptian bishops under Peter *"deposed him as a disturber of the peace of the church"*[244] (A.D. 306) for his irregular acts and insubordination. Athanasius[245] and Socrates[246] affirm indeed that the degradation of Meletius was specially due to his having *"denied the faith during persecution and sacrificed"*[247], but in this they probably express only the popular belief (which could not otherwise explain why orthodox bishops were imprisoned and martyred, while Meletius passed through the length and breadth of the land unhindered) and seems to be false and totally against the extremist position of the bishop of Lycopolis, who, on the contrary, with his group, later known with the name of "Church of the Martyrs", as said, had as reason to live the total objection to the re-acceptance by other bishops of people who chose to avoid the risk of martyrdom. Moreover, even the council bishops in their condemnation of Meletius, took no note of impiety so that the statement of Epiphanius[248]: "[Meletius] *was orthodox in his belief, and never dissented from the creed of the church in a single point. He was the author of a schism, but not of alterations of belief*", is probably true of the bishop, if not of his followers. Anyway, Meletius retorted upon his deposers by separating himself and his followers: Peter preached against the Meletians, and rejected their baptism[249]; Meletius retaliated by abusing Peter and his immediate successors Achillas and Alexander.

---

244) P.Schaff, *History of the Christian Church*, Vol.II, Sec. LVIII, Hendrickson Publishers 1885, p.306
245) Athanasius, *Epistulae*, II.5
246) Socrates Scholasticus, *Cit.*, II.3
247) *Ibidem*
248) Epiphanius Scholasticus, *Historiae Ecclesiasticae Tripartitae Epitome*, II.6
249) Sozomen, *Cit.*, I.15

The supporters that Melitius drew around him included twenty-eight other bishops, at least some of whom he personally ordained: the objections against him included that he ordained people in regions where he lacked authority, and, effectively, Melitius' influence extended even so far away as Palestine[250].

The council of Nicaea attempted to create peace with the Melitians: the line adopted was one of "clemency" and Meletius was permitted to remain in his own city and retain a nominal dignity, but was not to ordain or nominate for ordination.

Why such a difference with the treatment reserved to Arius? Simply as, as stated before, there was nothing theological in this dispute: Meletius was surely a very strict man, even an extremist in his positions, but was also a person who had suffered for his faith and who had always acted in favor of a purity (an even excessive purity) of the Church[251]. His schism had been provoked mainly by problems of political and hierarchic adjustment of a still young and not very well defined in its structures Church. It is, in fact, meaningful that the most important statement about his "sect" in the *Synodal Letter* is related to the fact that those who had received appointments from him had to be confirmed by a more legitimate ordination and then admitted to communion and retain their rank and ministry, but, and here we have the key point, were to be counted inferior to those previously ordained and established by Alexander (and Alexander was, in the end, one of the real winners in Nicea). Moreover, once again the council was moving in the direction wished by Constantine, who had all interests in passing the Melitian problem in a sort of understatement, as the whole matter was a little too much linked to the previous terrible relations between empire and Christianity to receive a too large space in a council which had

---

250) AA.VV., *Encyclopædia Britannica*, III, p. 288
251) A. Neander, *Church History*, Vol.II, CFT Schneider 1828, pp.211ff

to be a ratification of the new alliance between the two subjects. It is doubtful whether Meletius was at the council, but surely he did not resist its decrees. At Alexander's request he handed in a list of his clerical adherents, retired to Lycopolis, and during Alexander's lifetime remained quiet.

Only at the appointment of Athanasius to the see of Alexandria, which was, somehow, the signal for union of every faction opposed to him, Meletius came back to take part to the events that followed: the uncompromising sternness of Athanasius was contrasted with the "clemency" of the council and of Alexander, so Arians and Meletians, schismatic and heretic, banded together against the one man they dreaded, and so pitiless and powerful was their hate that it wrung from him the comment on the pardon accorded to Meletius by the council of Nicaea *"Would to God he had never been received!"*[252]

Before his death, the date of which is not known, Meletius nominated, contrary to the decree of the Nicene council, his friend John as his successor, a rank later accorded to him and recognized by that council of Tyre (A.D. 335) in which the Eusebians and others deposed Athanasius[253].

"In process of time", says Sozomen[254], *"the Meletians were generally called Arians in Egypt."*: originally differences in doctrine parted them but their alliance for attack or defence gradually led the Meletians to adopt Arian doctrines and side with Arian church politics, so that the Meletians died out only after the V century.

As for many other doctrinal points, the results of the council had been absolutely ineffective.

---

252) Sozomen, *Cit.*, II.21
253) *Ibidem*, II.25
254) *Ibidem*, II,21

Dr. Lawrence M.F. Sudbury – **Nicea: what it was, what it was not**

III.3) THE CANON, THE CHURCH AND THE CLERGY

As said, a canon is, fundamentally, a series of strict laws ruling the internal relations of the Church. The canon of the "Great Synod" (the way the participants to Nicea used to call the council) is, exactly like any other canon, simply this: a series of practical and pressing rules to use in different situations of the life of local churches, formalized mainly to give homogeneity to the behaviors of the single communities. The echo of the big troubles the synod (and the whole Church before it) had to face is quite clear in some of them, as well as the concern of the council fathers to condemn any form of heresy and schism and to find a common line in dealing with the adherents and former adherents to the different not orthodox ideas spread in the previous century, but, basically, no fundamental or theological rule is stated in this list of norms, mainly dealing with problems related to the clergy behavior and to local communities hierarchies and rules.

To understand how the aim of the Nicean Canon is mainly practical and linked to the circumstances of the time it is enough to explain and comment, one by one but very briefly, under the guide of the most important historical commentaries of the past centuries[255], the various directions it gives.

Canon 1: On the admission, or support, or expulsion of clerics mutilated by choice or by violence.[256]

The feeling that one devoted to the sacred ministry should be

---

255) Widely gathered by Philip Shaff and Henry Wance in P.Shaff, H.Wance, *Nicene and post-Nicene Fathers*, Series II, V. XIV, Wm. B. Eerdmans Puplishing Company 1994, passim

256) This and all short versions of the canons come from the ancient epitomes already present in the first known redactions of the texts.

unmutilated was strong in the ancient Church as many members of the clergy were moving towards that perverted notion of piety, originating in the misinterpretation of the Gospel[257] (by which Origen, among others, was misled), and the fighting against self-castration episodes was so carefully enforced in later times that not more than one or two instances of the practice condemned by this canon are noticed by the historians[258]. In example, we know, by the first apology of Justin[259], that a century before Origen, a young man had desired to be mutilated by physicians, for the purpose of completely refuting the charge of vice which the heathen brought against the worship of Christians. Justin neither praises nor blames this young man: he only relates that he could not obtain the permission of the civil authorities for his project and that he renounced his intention. It is very probable that the council of Nicea was induced by some fresh similar cases to renew the old injunctions and it was perhaps the Arian bishop, Leontius, who, admitting and even encouraging self-mutilation of the priests, was the principal cause of it[260]. Also Constantine forbade by a law the practice condemned in this canon: *"If anyone shall anywhere in the Roman empire after this decree make eunuchs, he shall be punished with death. If the owner of the place where the deed was perpetrated was aware of it and hid the fact, his goods shall be confiscated"*[261], which was later confirmed in the II council of Arles[262] and inserted in the *Corpus Juris Canonici*[263].

The case was obviously different if a man was born an eunuch

---

257) Mt. 19: 12
258) W.Smith, S.Cheetham, *Dictionary of Christian Antiquities*, Vol. 1, 11, John Murray 1875, p.176
259) Justin Martyr, *Apologia*, I.29
260) K.J. Von Hefele, *Cit.*, Vol. II., pp. 96ff
261) AA.VV., *Constini Magni Opera*, Migne Patrol., vol. VIII, 396
262) Canon VII
263) *Corpus Juris Canonici*, Decretum Gratiani. Pars. I. Distinctio LV., C. VII

or had suffered mutilation at the hands of persecutors: an instance of the former, Dorotheus, presbyter of Antioch, is mentioned by Eusebius[264] and an example of the latter, Tigris, presbyter of Constantinople, is referred both by Socrates[265] and Sozomen[266] as the victim of a barbarian master.

Canon 2: Rules to be observed for ordination, the avoidance of undue haste, the deposition of those guilty of a grave fault.

It may be seen by the very text of this canon, that it was already forbidden to baptize and to raise to the episcopate or to the priesthood anyone who had only been a catechumen for a short time: this injunction is in fact contained in the *Apostolical Canon*[267] and according to that, it is older than the council of Nicea. There have been, nevertheless, certain cases in which, for urgent reasons, an exception has been made to the rule of the council of Nicea (for instance, that of S. Ambrose)[268]. The canon of Nicea does not seem to allow such exceptions although they might be justified by the *Apostolical Canon* itself, which says, at the close: *"It is not right that anyone who has not yet been proved should be a teacher of others, unless by a peculiar divine grace."*

Canon 3: All members of the clergy are forbidden to dwell with any woman, except a mother, sister, or aunt.

As already Justellus[269] notes, who the "mulieres subintroductæ"[270] mentioned in the Latin version of the canon were is not very clear. Surely they were neither wives nor concubines, but women of some third kind, which the clergy

---

264) Eusebius of Caesarea, *Cit.*, VII.32
265) Socrates Scholasticus, *Cit.*, VI.15
266) Sozomen, *Cit.*, VI.24
267) *Apostolical Canon* LXXX
268) K.J. Von Hefele, *Cit.*, Vol. I., p. 308
269) Justellus, *Bibliotheca Juris Canonici*, Paris, 1661, II, 449ff
270) "Women hiddenly introduced"

kept with them, not for the sake of offspring or lust, but from the desire, or certainly under the pretence, of piety. It is very certain that the canon of Nicea forbids such spiritual unions, but the context shows moreover that the council fathers had not these particular cases in view alone: if we see[271] the "subintroductæ" as every woman who is introduced into the house of a clergyman for the purpose of living there, we should think that the practice of clerical celibacy had already spread widely[272].

Canon 4: Concerning episcopal elections.

The present canon might seem to be opposed to the first *Apostolic Canon*, which states a bishop must be ordained by two bishops while this one by three. Actually the two rules are not contradictory: the *Apostolical Canon* by ordination means consecration and imposition of hands, while the present canon by constitution and ordination means the election and enjoins that the election of a bishop can't take place unless three bishops assemble, or, at least, two, but having the consent also of a third absent bishop by letter[273]. In practice, the council of Nicea thought it necessary to define by precise rules the duties of the bishops who took part in these episcopal elections. It decided that a single bishop of the province was not sufficient for the appointment of another and that, moreover, the ordination by three bishops had to be obtained afterward the approval of the metropolitan. The council thus confirms the ordinary metropolitan division in its two most important points, namely, the nomination and ordination of bishops, and the superior position of the metropolitan[274].

Meletius, whose heresy and personal ordinations we just

---

271) As K.J. Von Hefele, *Cit.*, Vol. I., p. 310
272) As suggested by G.D.Fuchs, *Bibliothek der Kirchenver-sammlungen*, Leipsic, 1780-1784, Vol II, p.141
273) J.Zonaras, *Extracts of History*, II.8
274) K.J. Von Hefele, *Cit.*, Vol. I., p. 311

analyzed, was probably the occasion of this canon which was intended to prevent the recurrence of such abuses.

Canon 5: Concerning the excommunicate.

This is probably the least followed canon of Nicea. It states that excommunications could be raised by a synod, but the problem is that there has always been found the greatest difficulty in securing the regular meetings of provincial and diocesan synods, and despite the very explicit canonical legislation upon the subject and the severe penalties attached to those not answering the summons, in large parts of the Church, for centuries, these councils have been of the rarest occurrence (in example, Zonaras complains that in his time[275] synods had actually ceased to be held at all[276]). So, although the general idea of synods investigating about excommunications was stated (and maintained in the *Corpus Juris Canonici*[277]), it was practically unfeasible, meaning that the bishop who has passed the sentence of excommunication was also the only one having the right to mitigate it[278].

Canon 6: Concerning patriarchs and their jurisdiction.

Many, probably most, commentators have considered this the most important and most interesting of all the Nicene canons, and a whole library of works has been written upon it, some of the works asserting and some denying what are commonly called the "Papal claims". Anyway, the object and intention of this canon seems clearly to have been not to introduce any new powers or regulations into the Church, but to confirm and establish ancient customs already existing. This, indeed, is evident from the very first words of it: "*Let the ancient customs be maintained.*" It appears to have been made with particular

---

275) XII century
276) J.Zonaras, *Extracts of History*, III.3
277) *Corpus Juris Canonici*, Gratian's Decretum, Pars II., Causa XI, Quæst. III., Canon LXIII
278) K.J. Von Hefele, *Cit.*, Vol. I., p. 312

reference to the case of the church of Alexandria, which had been troubled by the irregular proceedings of Meletius, and to confirm the ancient privileges of that see which he had invaded. The problematic point was the inclusion of the sentence about Rome. It is on this clause (*"since the like is customary for the Bishops of Rome also"*), standing parenthetically between what is decreed for the particular cases of Egypt and Antioch, and in consequence of the interpretation given to it by Rufinus[279] (who, being from Aquileia could have misrepresented the whole situation on purpose to favor the Roman see) more particularly, that so much strife has been raised[280].

Canon 7: confirms the right of the bishops of Jerusalem to enjoy certain honours.

There would seem to be a singular fitness in the "Holy City Jerusalem" holding a very exalted position among the sees of Christendom, and it may appear astonishing that in the earliest times it was only a suffragan see to the great Church of Cesarea. It must be remembered, however, that only about seventy years after Jesus' death the city of Jerusalem was entirely destroyed and "ploughed as a field" according to the biblical prophecy. As a holy city Jerusalem had been a thing of the past for long years, and it was only in the beginning of the II century that we find a strong Christian Church growing up in the rapidly increasing city, called no longer Jerusalem, but Ælia Capitolina. Possibly by the end of the II century the idea of the holiness of the site began to lend dignity to the occupant of the see. At all events, Eusebius tells us that *"at a synod held on the subject of the Easter controversy in the time of Pope Victor, Theophilus of Cæsarea and Narcissus of Jerusalem were presidents."*[281]

It was this feeling of reverence which induced the passing of

---

279) Rufinus of Aquileia (*Cit.*) sees this canon as a confirm of the supremacy of Rome among all bishop sees
280) F. Ffoulkes, *Dict. Christ. Antiq.*, Entry "Council of Nicæa"
281) Eusebius of Caesarea, *Cit.*, V.32

this seventh canon. It is very hard to determine just what was the "precedence" granted to the Bishop of Ælia, nor is it clear which is the metropolis referred to in the last clause (most writers consider it to be Cæsarea; while others think about Jerusalem or even Antioch).

Canon 8: concerns the Novatians.

The Cathari or Novatians were the followers of Novatian, a presbyter of Rome, who had been a Stoic philosopher and was delivered, according to his own story, from diabolical possession at his exorcising by the Church before his baptism, when becoming a catechumen. Being in peril of death by illness he received clinical baptism, and was ordained priest without any further sacred rites being administered to him. During the persecution he constantly refused to assist his brethren, and afterwards raised his voice against what he considered their culpable laxity in admitting to penance the lapsed. Many agreed with him in this, especially among the clergy, and eventually, in A.D. 251, he induced three bishops to consecrate him, thus becoming, as already Fleury remarks[282], "the first Anti-Pope." His indignation was principally spent upon Pope Cornelius and, to overthrow the prevailing discipline of the Church, he ordained bishops and sent them to different parts of the empire as the disseminators of his ideas. It is well to remember that while beginning only as a schismatic, he soon fell into heresy, denying that the Church had the power to absolve the lapsed. Although condemned by several councils his sect continued on, and like the Montanists they rebaptized Catholics who apostatized to them[283]. At the time of the council of Nicea a Novatian bishop at Constantinople, Acesius, was greatly esteemed, and although a schismatic, was, as seen, invited to

---

282) M. B. C. Fleury, *Histoire ecclésiastique*, Paris, Mariette, 1691-1738, VI.53
283) R.J.DeSimone, *The treatise of Novatian, the Roman presbyter on the Trinity: A Study of the Text and the Doctrine*. Studia Ephemeridis "Augustinianum", 1970, passim

attend the council. After having, in an answer to the emperor's enquiry whether he was willing to sign the creed, assured him that he was, he went on to explain that his separation was because the Church no longer observed the ancient discipline which forbade that those who had committed mortal sin should ever be readmitted to communion. According to the Novatians they might be exhorted to repentance, but the Church had no power to assure them of forgiveness and had to leave them to the judgment of God. It was then that Constantine, as mentioned speaking about the events of the council, joked him saying, *"Acesius, take a ladder, and climb up to heaven alone."*[284]

Canon 9: Certain sins known after ordination involve invalidation.

According to Hefele[285], the crimes invalidating the ordination are those which were commonly considered a bar to the priesthood (such as blasphemy, bigamy, heresy, idolatry, magic, etc.). It is clear that these faults are punishable in the bishop no less than in the priest, and that consequently this canon refers to the bishops as well as to the presbyters in the more restricted sense. These words of the Greek text, *"In the case in which any one might be induced, in opposition to the canon, to ordain such persons,"* allude to the IX canon[286] of the synod of Neocæsarea[287]. It was necessary to pass such ordinances for even in the fifth century, as the *XXII Letter to Pope Innocent* testifies, some held that as baptism effaced all former sins, so it took away all the "impedimenta ordinationis" which are the results of those sins.

---

284) Sozomen, *Cit.*, II
285) K.J. Von Hefele, *Cit.*, Vol. I., p. 318
286) *"A presbyter who has been promoted after having committed carnal sin, and who shall confess that he had sinned before his ordination, shall not make the oblation, though he may remain in his other functions on account of his zeal in other respects; for the majority have affirmed that ordination blots out other kinds of sins. But if he do not confess and cannot be openly convicted, the decision shall depend upon himself"*.
287) Held in A.D. 315

Canon 10: Lapsi who have been ordained knowingly or surreptitiously must be excluded as soon as their irregularity is known.

The tenth canon differs from the ninth uniquely as it concerns just the "lapsi" and their elevation, not only to the priesthood, but to any other ecclesiastical preferment as well, and requires their deposition. The punishment of a bishop who should consciously perform such an ordination is not mentioned, but it is incontestable that the lapsi could not be ordained, even after having performed penance, for, as the preceding canon states, the Church requires those who were faultless.

Canon 11: Penance to be imposed on apostates of the persecution of Licinius.

Public penance for apostates was a general institution for a short while in the Church and, according to the seriousness of their apostasy and to the circumstances leading to it, these apostates were divided into different categories[288]. The most important of them were the "hearers" (actually a stage of the cathecumenal process) and the "prostrators".

The usual position of the hearers was just inside the church door, but Zonaras, in his comment on this canon, says, *"they are ordered for three years to be hearers, or to stand without the church in the narthex."*[289]. The prostrators, normally punished for inferior sins, stood within the body of the church behind the the reading desk and went out with the catechumens.

Canon 12: Penance to be imposed on those who upheld Licinius in his war on the Christians.

As we have seen, in his last contests with Constantine, Licinius had made himself the representative of paganism; so that the final issue of the war would not be the mere triumph of one of

---

288) For the different categories of the penitents see commentary to Canon 14
289) Zonaras, *Cit.*, III.7

the two competitors, but the triumph or fall of Christianity or heathenism. Accordingly, a Christian who had in this war supported the cause of Licinius and of heathenism might be considered as a lapsus, even if he did not formally fall away. With much more reason might be treated as lapsi those Christians who, having conscientiously given up military service, afterwards retracted their resolution, and went so far as to give money and presents for the sake of readmission, on account of the numerous advantages which military service then afforded. It must not be forgotten that Licinius, as Eusebius relates[290], required from his soldiers a formal apostasy and, for example, compelled them to take part in the heathen sacrifices which were held in the camps, dismissing from his service those who would not apostatize[291].

Canon 13: Indulgence to be granted to excommunicated persons in danger of death.

Although antiquity used the name "Viaticum" not only to denote the Eucharist which was given to the dying, but also to denote the reconciliation and imposition of penance, and in general, everything that could be conducive to the happy death of the person concerned[292], the most usual sense of the word is related to the Eucharist given near to the death. The believers of the first ages of the Church looked upon the Eucharist as the complement of Christian perfection and as the last seal of hope and salvation. It was for this reason that, at the beginning of life, after baptism and confirmation, the Eucharist was given even to infants, and at the close of life the Eucharist followed reconciliation and extreme unction, so that properly and literally it could be styled as "the last Viaticum." Moreover, for penitents it was considered especially necessary that, through it,

---

290) Eusebius of Caesarea, *Vita Constantini*, II.31ff
291) K.J. Von Hefele, *Cit.*, Vol. I., p. 324
292) As clear in G. Aubespine, *De veteribus Ecclesiae ritibus, observationum libri II*, Expensis Gregorii P. & Michaelis F. Stasi, 1770, I.2

they might return to the peace of the Church and this is the reason for this canonic imposition of indulgence even to excommunicated people.

Canon 14: Penance to be imposed on catechumens who had weakened under persecution.

According to Justellus[293], the people formerly were divided into three classes in the church, for there were catechumens, faithful, and penitents; but it is clear from the present canon that there were two kinds of catechumens: one consisting of those who heard the word of God, and wished to become Christians, but had not yet desired baptism, called "hearers", and others who were of long standing, were properly trained in the faith, desired baptism and were called "Competentes."

There is difference of opinion among scholars as to whether there was not a third or even a fourth class of catechumens. Bingham[294], in example, affirms that there were more than two classes. Bingham's first class was formed by those not allowed to enter the church, the "Exotsumenoi", but the affirmation of the existence of such a class rests only on a very forced explanation of canon five of Neocæsarea[295]. The second class, the one of the hearers or "Audientes", rests on better evidence. These were not allowed to stay while the Holy Mysteries were celebrated (and their expulsion gave rise to the distinction between the "Mass of the Catechumens" or "Missa Catechumenorum" and the "Mass of the Faithful" or "Missa

---

293) Justellus, *Cit.*, II, 483ff
294) J. Bingham, *The Antiquities of the Christian Church*, Oxford University Press, 1855, V.1
295) *"If a catechumen coming into the Church have taken his place in the order of catechumens, and fall into sin, let him, if a kneeler, become a hearer and sin no more. But should he again sin while a hearer, let him be cast out."*

Fidelium"), nor were they suffered to hear the creed or the Our Father. Writers who multiply the classes insert here some who knelt and prayed, called "Prostrati" or "Genuflectentes" (the same name as was given to one of the grades of penitence).

After these stages had been traversed each with its appropriate instruction, the catechumens, always according to Bingham, gave in their names as applicants for baptism and were known, accordingly, as "Competentes". This was done commonly at the beginning of the Quadragesimal fast and the instruction, carried on through the whole of that period, was fuller and more public in its nature. To catechumens, in this stage, the great articles of the creed, the nature of the Sacraments, the penitential discipline of the Church, were explained with dogmatic precision. Special examinations and inquiries into character were made at intervals during the forty days the preparation lasted. It was a time for fasting and watching and prayer and, in the case of those who were married, of the strictest continence. Those who passed through the ordeal were known as the "Perfectiores", "Electi", or, in the nomenclature of the Eastern Church, as "Baptizomenoi". Their names were inscribed as such in the album or register of the church. They were taught, but not till a few days before their baptism, the whole creed and the Lord's Prayer which they were to use after it. The periods for this registration varied, naturally enough, in different churches.

Canon 15: Bishops, priests, and deacons are not to pass from one church to another.

The translation of a bishop, priest or deacon from one church to another had already been forbidden in the primitive Church. Nevertheless, several translations had taken place, and even at the council of Nicea several eminent men were present who had left their first bishoprics to take others: thus Eusebius, Bishop of Nicomedia, had been before Bishop of Berytus; Eustathius, Bishop of Antioch, had been before Bishop of Berrhœa in Syria, etc.. The council of Nicea thought it necessary to forbid in future these translations and to declare them invalid. The chief reason of this prohibition was found in the irregularities and disputes occasioned by such change of sees; but even if such practical difficulties had not arisen, the whole doctrinal idea, so to speak, of the relationship between a cleric and the church to which he had been ordained, namely, the contracting of a mystical marriage between them, would be opposed to any translation or change. In A.D. 341 the synod of Antioch renewed, in its XXI canon[296], the prohibition passed by the council of Nicea; but the interest of the Church often rendered it necessary to make exceptions. These exceptional cases increased almost immediately after the holding of the council of Nicea, so that in A.D. 382, Gregory of Nazianzum considered this law among those which had long been abrogated by custom. It was more strictly observed in the Latin Church and even Gregory's contemporary, Pope Damasus, declared himself decidedly in favor of the rule established in Nicea[297].

Canon 16: All clerics are forbidden to leave their church. Formal prohibition for bishops to ordain for their diocese a cleric belonging to another diocese.

The medieval scholar Balsamon commented that it seemed right that the clergy should have no power to move from city to city and to change their canonical residence without dimissory letters from the bishop who ordained them. But such clerics, in the moment they were called by the bishops who had ordained them and couldn't be persuaded to return, had to be separated from communion (that is to say, not to be allowed to

---

296) *"A bishop may not be translated from one parish to another, either intruding himself of his own suggestion, or under compulsion by the people, or by constraint of the bishops; but he shall remain in the Church to which he was allotted by God from the beginning, and shall not be translated from it, according to the decree formerly passed on the subject"*.
297) K.J. Von Hefele, *Cit.*, Vol. I., pp. 341ff

concelebrate, and this is the meaning of "excommunicated" in this place, and not that they should not enter the church nor receive the sacraments). This decree agrees with canon XV of the *Apostolical Canons*, which provides that such shall not celebrate the liturgy. The canon XVI of the same *Apostolical Canons* further provides that if a bishop received a cleric coming to him from another diocese without his bishop's dimissory letters, and ordained him, such a bishop had to be separated too[298].

Canon 17: Clerics are forbidden to lend at interest.

Although the canon expresses only two species of usury, if we bear in mind the grounds on which the prohibition was made it will be manifest that every kind of usury is forbidden to clerics and under any circumstances, so much that in the version of the canon later reviewed by the VI council of Carthage[299] no mention is made of any particular kind of usury, but generally the penalty is assigned to any clerics who *"shall be found after this decree taking usury"* or thinking out any other scheme for the sake of filthy lucre[300].

Canon 18: recalls to deacons their subordinate position with regard to priests.

This canon condemns, at least indirectly, four excesses of the deacons. The first was that they gave the holy Communion to presbyters. To understand more easily the meaning of the canon it must be remembered that the reference here is not to the presbyters who were sacrificing at the altar but to those who were offering together with the bishop who was sacrificing: this rite in old times was of daily occurrence. The present canon does not take away from deacons the authority to distribute the Eucharist to laymen or to the minor clergy, but only reproves

---

298) T.Balsamon, *Scholia*, II.11
299) In A.D. 402
300) Z.B. Van Espen, *Tractatus Historicus exhibens scholia in omnes canones conciliorum...*, Louvain, 1753, I.17

their insolence and audacity in presuming to administer to presbyters who were concelebrating with the bishop or another presbyter.

The second abuse was that certain deacons touched the sacred gifts before the bishop.

"*Let them receive the Eucharist according to their order, after the presbyters, and let the bishop or the presbyter administer to them*": in these words it is implied that some deacons had presumed to receive Holy Communion before the presbyters, and this is the third excess of the deacons which is condemned by the synod. And lastly, the fourth excess was that they took a place among the presbyters at the very time of the sacrifice, or "at the holy altar".

But for the merely hierarchic problem, fixing a hierarchy in the Church, made up of bishops and presbyters and deacons in subordination to these[301], what is particularly interesting is that from this canon we see that the Nicene fathers entertained no doubt that the faithful in the holy Communion truly received "the body of Christ", so stating a fixed point in relation to the concept of transubstantiation.

Canon 19: Rules to be observed with regard to adherents of Paul of Samosata who wished to return to the Church.

By Paulianists, as seen, must be understood the followers of Paul of Samosata the anti-Trinitarian who, about A.D. 260, had been made bishop of Antioch but had been deposed by a great synod in A.D. 269. As Paul of Samosata was heretical in his teaching on the Holy Trinity the synod of Nicea simply applied to him the decree passed by the council of Arles in its VIII canon[302].

---

301) *Ibidem*, I.18

302) "*If anyone shall come from heresy to the Church, they shall ask him to say the creed; and if they shall perceive that he was baptized into the Father, and the Son, and the Holy Ghost, 102 he shall have a hand laid on him only that he may receive the Holy Ghost. But if in answer to their questioning he shall not answer this Trinity, let him be*

The Samosatans, in fact, according to St. Athanasius[303], named the Father, Son and Holy Spirit in administering baptism, but as they gave a false meaning to the baptismal formula and did not use the words Son and Holy Spirit in the usual sense, the council of Nicea, like St. Athanasius himself, considered their baptism as invalid.

Canon 20: On Sundays and during the Paschal season prayers should be said standing.

Although kneeling was the common posture for prayer in the primitive Church, yet the custom had prevailed, even from the earliest times, of standing at prayer on the Lord's day, and during the fifty days between Easter and Pentecost. Tertullian[304] mentions this amongst other observances which, though not expressly commanded in Scriptures, yet were universally practised upon the authority of tradition. *"We consider it unlawful,"* he says, *"to fast, or to pray kneeling, upon the Lord's day; we enjoy the same liberty from Easter-day to that of Pentecost."*. Many others among the Church fathers noticed the same practice, the reason of which, as given by Augustine and others, was to commemorate the resurrection of Christ and to signify the rest and joy of the resurrection. This canon is a proof of the importance formerly attached to a uniformity of sacred rites throughout the Church, which made the Nicene fathers thus sanction and enforce by their authority a practice which in itself is indifferent, and not commanded directly or indirectly in Scriptures, and explain their reason for doing so with these words: *"In order that all things may be observed in like manner in every parish"* or diocese[305].

---

baptized."
303) Athanasius, *Oratio II Contra Arian.*, XLIII
304) Tertulianus, *De Corona Militis*, III.4
305) A.Hammond, *The Definitions of Faith and Canons of Discipline of the Six*

Hierarchies, procedures, punishments and readmissions: this is all the twenty canons of Nicea finally give us. They can seem to us a little lacking in feeling, but, clearly, all these elements were fundamental for the institution of a unitarian Church. And unity, as seen, was the central item in Nicea, not only to avoid further heretic ramifications of the core believes, but also in relation to the newly attested deep link Christianity was developing with the empire: in the imperial vision, if Christianity had to be an element of spiritual and political unity for the Roman areas, it was essential that it had to be at least homogeneous inside of its own body.

Œcumenical Councils, Oxford University Press 1879, pp.137-138

Dr. Lawrence M.F. Sudbury – **Nicea: what it was, what it was not**

III.4) CONSTANTINE'S LETTERS

Possibly, one of the elements most clearly showing the importance attributed by the emperor to the results of the council is given by the many letters he wrote after the synod to be certain all the instructions and decisions of the bishops were going to be followed scrupulously.
Just to briefly analyze a few of them will be enough to see this point
A first long missive, already mentioned in a short quotation in the previous chapters, is a sort of circular letter about the Easter festivity, sent to all the churches of the empire immediately after the end of the formal meeting and even before the final banquet. The text, as received by Eusebius and Socrates[306], sounds as follows.
"Having had full proof, in the general prosperity of the empire, how great the favor of God has been towards us, I have judged that it ought to be the first object of my endeavors, that unity of faith, sincerity of love, and community of feeling in regard to the worship of Almighty God, might be preserved among the highly favored multitude who compose the Catholic Church. And, inasmuch as this object could not be effectually and certainly secured, unless all, or at least the greater number of the bishops were to meet together, and a discussion of all particulars relating to our most holy religion to take place; for this reason as numerous an assembly as possible has been convened, at which I myself was present, as one among yourselves (and far be it from me to deny that which is my greatest joy, that I am your fellow-servant), and every question received due and full examination, until that judgment which God, who sees all things, could approve, and which tended to unity and concord, was brought to light, so that no room was left for further discussion or controversy in relation to the faith. "AT this meeting the question concerning the most holy day of Easter was discussed,

---

306) Eusebius of Caesarea, *Life of Constantine*, 3:17–20 and Socrates Scholasticus, *Cit.*, 1:9

and it was resolved by the united judgment of all present, that this feast ought to be kept by all and in every place on one and the same day. For what can be more becoming or honorable to us than that this feast from which we date our hopes of immortality, should be observed unfailingly by all alike, according to one ascertained order and arrangement? And first of all, it appeared an unworthy thing that in the celebration of this most holy feast we should follow the practice of the Jews, who have impiously defiled their hands with enormous sin, and are, therefore, deservedly afflicted with blindness of soul. For we have it in our power, if we abandon their custom, to prolong the due observance of this ordinance to future ages, by a truer order, which we have preserved from the very day of the passion until the present time. Let us then have nothing in common with the detestable Jewish crowd; for we have received from our Saviour a different way. A course at once legitimate and honorable lies open to our most holy religion. Beloved brethren, let us with one consent adopt this course, and withdraw ourselves from all participation in their baseness. For their boast is absurd indeed, that it is not in our power without instruction from them to observe these things. For how should they be capable of forming a sound judgment, who, since their parricidal guilt in slaying their Lord, have been subject to the direction, not of reason, but of ungoverned passion, and are swayed by every impulse of the mad spirit that is in them? Hence it is that on this point as well as others they have no perception of the truth, so that, being altogether ignorant of the true adjustment of this question, they sometimes celebrate Easter twice in the same year. Why then should we follow those who are confessedly in grievous error? Surely we shall never consent to keep this feast a second time in the same year. But supposing these reasons were not of sufficient weight, still it would be incumbent on your Sagacities to strive and pray continually that the purity of your souls may not seem in anything to be sullied by fellowship with the customs of these most wicked men. We must consider, too, that a discordant judgment in a case of such importance, and respecting such religious festival, is wrong. For our Saviour has left us one feast in commemoration of the day of our deliverance, I mean the day of his most holy passion; and he has willed that his Catholic Church should be one, the members of which, however scattered in many and diverse places, are yet cherished by one pervading spirit, that is, by the will of God. And let your Holinesses' sagacity reflect how grievous and scandalous it is that on the self-same days some should be engaged in fasting, others in festive enjoyment; and again, that after the days of Easter some should be present at banquets and amusements, while others are fulfilling the appointed fasts. It is, then, plainly the will of Divine Providence (as I suppose you all clearly see), that this usage should receive fitting correction, and be reduced to one uniform rule. "Since, therefore, it was needful that this matter should be rectified, so that we might have nothing in common with that nation of parricides who slew their Lord: and since that arrangement is consistent with propriety which is observed by all the churches of the western, southern, and northern parts of the world, and by some of the eastern also: for these reasons all are unanimous on this present occasion in thinking it worthy of adoption. And I myself have undertaken that this decision should meet with the approval of your Sagacities, in the hope that your Wisdoms will gladly admit that practice which is observed at once in the city of Rome, and in Africa; throughout Italy, and in Egypt, in Spain, the Gauls, Britain, Libya, and the whole of Greece; in the dioceses of Asia and Pontus, and in Cilicia, with entire unity of judgment. And you will consider not only that the number of churches is far greater in the regions I have enumerated than in any other, but also that it is most fitting that all should unite in desiring that which sound reason appears to demand, and in avoiding all participation in the perjured conduct of the Jews. In fine, that I may express my meaning in as few words as possible, it has been determined by the common judgment of all, that the most holy feast of Easter should be kept on one and the same day. For on the one hand a discrepancy of opinion on so sacred a question is unbecoming, and on the other it is surely best to act on a decision which is free from strange folly and error.

RECEIVE, then, with all willingness this truly Divine injunction, and regard it as in truth the gift of God. For whatever is determined in the holy assemblies of the bishops is to be regarded as indicative of the Divine will. As soon, therefore, as you have communicated these proceedings to all our beloved brethren, you are bound from that time forward to adopt for yourselves, and to enjoin on others the arrangement above mentioned, and the due observance of this most sacred day; that whenever I come into the presence of your love, which I have long desired, I may have it in my power to celebrate the holy feast with you on the same day, and may rejoice with you on all accounts, when I behold the cruel power of Satan removed by Divine aid through the agency of our endeavors, while your faith, and peace, and concord everywhere flourish. God preserve you, beloved brethren."

What we can see at a glance is that, but for the core message about Easter celebration, three main elements absorb a great part of the letter.

A first element is given by the repeated and continuous warning to the need for unity: unity of faith and worshiping, but also unity (which actually didn't exist in reality) among the bishops in the moment of their decisions are underlined practically at any paragraph, so that it's quite clear that, much more than the rebuttal of any heretic thought, this global cohesion of the Christian Church is actually what Constantine was willing for (and we've already seen that it was necessary to him mainly for political reasons).

The second quite evidently emerging element is that the emperor firmly states his position towards the Church and towards the synodal bylaws, in two different forms. At the beginning he, somehow, wheedles the local churches leaders reminding them the high favor he deserves to the Christians and showing an even abnormal humility and devotion towards Christianity, but, mainly towards the end of the missive, he finely and progressively changes his tone, both stressing his "imprimatur" on the council decisions and pushing (almost ordering and even ventilating the possibility of personal controls) to obey them. In a certain sense he states the fact of being the guarantor of the actuation of the bishops' deliberations, giving way to a first step of the determination of roles typical of the "caesaropapism".

Finally, a third element clearly stated by the letter is the anti-Judaism we already spoke about in other parts of this research. Once again, it is important to state that this position is totally political: Constantine is simply giving voice to a diffused feeling, widely present in the Christian churches, and, therefore, he is affirming his adherence to the Christian way of thinking, choosing a sure allied and strengthening this alliance by despising a "common enemy"[307].

The second letter we can read to have a clear opinion of the position of the emperor is the one sent, again in A.D.325, in the month following the end of the council, to the church of Alexandria, which had been the spring of the Arian Controversy.

"Beloved brethren, hail! We have received from Divine Providence the inestimable blessing of being relieved from all error, and united in the acknowledgment of one and the same faith. The devil will no longer have any power against us, since all that which he had malignantly devised for our destruction has been entirely overthrown from the foundations. The splendor of truth has dissipated at the command of God those dissensions, schisms, tumults and so to speak, deadly poisons of discord. Wherefore we all worship one true God, and believe that he is. But in order that this might be done, by divine admonition I assembled at the city of Nicaea most of the bishops; with whom I myself also, who am but one of you, and who rejoice exceedingly in being your fellow-servant, undertook the investigation of the truth. Accordingly, all points which seemed in consequence of ambiguity to furnish any pretext for dissension, have been discussed and accurately examined. And may the Divine Majesty pardon the fearful enormity of the blasphemies which some were shamelessly uttering concerning the mighty Saviour, our life and hope; declaring and confessing that they believe things contrary to the divinely inspired Scriptures. While more than three hundred bishops remarkable for their moderation and

---

307) J.Carrol, *Constantine's Sword. The Church and the Jews: A History*, Houghton Mifflin, 2001, pp.421ff.

intellectual keenness, were unanimous in their confirmation of one and the same faith, which according to the truth and legitimate construction of the law of God can only be the faith; Arius alone beguiled by the subtlety of the devil was discovered to be the sole disseminator of this mischief, first among you, and afterward with unhallowed purposes among others also. Let us therefore embrace that doctrine which the Almighty has presented to us: let us return to our beloved brethren from whom an irreverent servant of the devil has separated us: let us go with all speed to the common body and our own natural members. For this is becoming your penetration, faith and sanctity; that since the error has been proved to be due to him who is an enemy to the truth, ye should return to the divine favor. For that which has commended itself to the judgment of three hundred bishops cannot be other than the doctrine of God; seeing that the Holy Spirit dwelling in the minds of so many dignified persons has effectually enlightened them respecting the Divine will. Wherefore let no one vacillate or linger, but let all with alacrity return to the undoubted path of duty; that when I shall arrive among you, which will be as soon as possible, I may with you return due thanks to God, the inspector of all things, for having revealed the pure faith, and restored to you that love for which ye have prayed. May God protect you, beloved brethren."[308]

As we can see, we are in front of a masterpiece of political ability. Once again, Constantine stresses in multiple passages the need for unity and his position towards the Church, this time tributing directly to himself the initiative to summon the council. Once again he presents himself as a devote Christian, acting for the good of the Church and possibly controlling the appliance of the council decrees. But, even not keeping into account that Constantine, as seen, was almost surely not a Christian, what is really shocking in this letter is the harsh position he takes against Arius. This last is seen as an instrument of the devil, whose heresy must be uprooted. There is only a problem in all this statement: the fact that the bishop

---

308) Socrates Scholasticus, *Ecclesiastical History*, 1:9

of Nicomedia, Eusebius, was one of the most strenuous supporters of Arius and that Constantine will have absolutely no problem in receiving the baptism (always if it's true he ever received it) from this Arian priest, who all along his life, with a short parenthesis in which the graces of the emperor moved to Hosius, acted as the imperial religious guide ...

A similar situation can be found in a further short letter dated to the same year and addressed to all the churches and the prefects to deal directly with the extirpation of the heresies.

"*Constantine the King to the Bishops and nations everywhere.*
Inasmuch as Arius imitates the evil and the wicked, it is right that, like them, he should be rebuked and rejected. As therefore Porphyry, who was an enemy of the fear of God, and wrote wicked and unlawful writings against the religion of Christians, found the reward which befitted him, that he might be a reproach to all generations after, because he fully and insatiably used base fame; so that on this account his writings were righteously destroyed; thus also now it seems good that Arius and the holders of his opinion should all be called Porphyrians, that he may be named by the name of those whose evil ways he imitates: And not only this, but also that all the writings of Arius, wherever they be found, shall be delivered to be burned with fire, in order that not only his wicked and evil doctrine may be destroyed, but also that the memory of himself and of his doctrine may be blotted out, that there may not by any means remain to him remembrance in the world. Now this also I ordain, that if any one shall be found secreting any writing composed by Arius, and shall |7 not forthwith deliver up and burn it with fire, his punishment shall be death; for as soon as he is caught in this he shall suffer capital punishment by beheading without delay."[309]

In this missive, Constantine gets completely unveiled. We must remember that, as we will see in next section, the orders of

---

309) Preserved in Socrates Scholasticus, *Ecclesiastical History*, 1:9. A translation of a Syriac translation of this, written in A.D. 501, is in B. H. Cowper, *Syriac Miscellanies, Extracts From The Syriac Ms. No. 14528 In The British Museum*, London 1861, p. 6–7

Nicea council passed by largely unheard, frustrating the imperial aims. So the tone changes radically, from the very beginning: the emperor now speaks no more as a presumed believer worried about the unity of the church, but assumes his role of "king" back and gives orders both to bishops and secular functionaries to act in a sort of "damnatio memoriae" of both Arius and Porphyry (a neoplatonic or neopythagorean philosopher we have very scarce information about, but for the fact he denied the possibility of purification from the sins through the baptism[310]) and to destroy all the writings of these authors. His position is now clearly caesaro-papistic in all senses, foreshadowing the alliance between Church and secular power which will make of the latter the "armed force" of Christianity.

The asset of the "do ut des" relation between orthodoxy and empire is now completely formed: the empire asks (and imposes) cohesion and unitarian support to a Church, which, in exchange, receives favor and protection thanks to all the powers (even the juridical and military one) of the emperor. Both obtain what they want: Constantine gets the strength of an expanding spiritual body standing on his side, the Church the support (even a too invading support) of the temporal authority to be protected and to solve its internal problems. And, actually, there is nothing spiritual in this alliance: it is just the political product of the staggering times the empire is living on one side and of the still unstable situation of a growing Church on the other side. It could have been a profitable deal for both parts, if things would have worked the way Constantine had projected.

Some people, even scholars[311], think the Church obtained the base of its actual configuration thanks to its first ecumenical council and to the assumption by Constantine of the role of

---

310) I.McGregor, *The Enemies of the Church Are my Enemies. The Rootes of the alliance between Church and empire*, Colton Press, 2002, pp. 47-49
311) In example: A.Borman, *The Church of the First Centuries*, Alkemia, 2004 passim

protector of the Christianity.
Actually, things didn't work this way and this is just one of the many misunderstanding surrounding the synod of Nicea.

Dr. Lawrence M.F. Sudbury – **Nicea: what it was, what it was not**

IV

PERPLEXITIES AND MISTAKES

Dr. Lawrence M.F. Sudbury – **Nicea: what it was, what it was not**

IV.1) WHERE IS THE CANON?

Before analyzing the immediate results of the council of Nicea on the situation of the Church and of the empire, it is fundamental to clean the field out from one of the most common but also of the grossest mistakes related to the synod: the one related to the Evangelical canon.
At the beginning of this essay, we saw *The Da Vinci Code* to have a look to some of the most diffused opinions about what happened in the council. In the same book we can find also these statements:
"To fully understand the Grail, we must first understand the Bible [...] *The Bible did not arrive by fax from heaven* [... it] *is a product of man* [...] *not God* [...] *and it has evolved through countless translations, additions and revisions. History never had a definitive version of the book.* [...] *Jesus Christ was a historical figure of staggering influence* [...] *his life was recorded by thousands of followers ... More than eighty gospels were considered for the New Testament, and yet only a relative few were chosen for inclusion — Matthew, Mark, Luke, and John among them"* and *"[...]Constantine commissioned and financed a new Bible, which omitted those gospels that spoke of Christ's human traits and embellished those gospels that made Him godlike. The earlier gospels were outlawed, gathered up, and burned* [...] *Who chose which gospels to include?* [...] *The Bible, as we know it today, was collated by the pagan Roman emperor Constantine"*.
In the previous chapters we have read and analyzed the elements discussed in the council of Nicea and the important role of Constantine in the first ecumenical synod of the Christianity. The natural question which immediately comes to our mind is: where is the canon? No trace of any discussion about the canonical writings emerges from any of the reports of the meeting and the reason is simply that actually the Evangelical canon was absolutely not in the council agenda.

The point is that, as McDowell remarks[312], the Church had recognized the majority of the books forming the definitive New Testament already 200 years before Nicea but this choice was formalized in the 27 Books we know only in AD.393, in another council, the one of Hippo.

The council of Nicea had nothing to deal with this choice and to understand this we need to have a brief excursus on the formation of the canon, going, once again, a little back in time.

The period immediately following the passing of the apostles, known as the period of the Church fathers, saw the presence of many men who had walked with the apostles and had been taught directly by them. Doctrinal authority during this period rested on two sources, the Old Testament and the notion of "apostolic succession", being able to trace a direct association to one of the apostles and thus to Christ. Although the New Testament canon Books were already written, they were not yet seen as a separate body of Books equivalent to the Old Testament. Six church leaders are commonly referred to as the collectors of all these writings: Barnabas, Hermas, Clement of Rome, Polycarp, Papias, and Ignatius[313]. Although these men lacked the technical sophistication of today's theologians, their correspondence confirmed the teachings of the apostles and provides a doctrinal link to nowadays New Testament canon itself. But we need to think that Christianity was as yet a fairly small movement and that these Church fathers, often elders and bishops in the early Church, were consumed by the practical aspects of Christian life among the new converts: there had been neither time nor necessity to focus on the issue of the canon. They had no doubt about the authority of the Old Testament and, as a result, they tended to be rather moralistic

---

312) J.McDowell, *Da Vinci Code: A Quest for Answers*, Green Key Books, 2006, p.42

313) L. Berkhof, *The History of Christian Doctrines*, Banner of Truth, 1996, p.37

and even legalistic on some issues, using this viewpoint also in the choice of some of the texts included in church lectures: so, as a fixed New Testament canon was not yet settled, they respected (and quoted from) works that have generally passed out of the Christian tradition, such as the books of *Hermas, Barnabas, Didaché*, and *1 and 2* Clement[314]. Although some of these early Church fathers may seem today rather ill-prepared to hand down all the subtle implications of the Christian faith to the coming generations, they formed a doctrinal link to the apostles, as well as a witness to the growing commitment to the future canon of Scriptures that would become the New Testament.

Almost ironically, the process of "scientifically" collecting and consolidating Scriptures was launched only when the Marcionite sect produced its own quasi-biblical canon. Around A.D. 140, according to his idea that the New and Old Testaments didn't share the same God, Marcion rejected the Old Testament and the most overtly Jewish New Testament writings, including Matthew, Mark, Acts, and Hebrews, while manipulating other books to downplay their Jewish tendencies. Although in A.D. 144 the church in Rome declared his views heretical, Marcion's teaching, as seen, sparked a new cult and, challenged by the Marcion's threat, church leaders began to consider earnestly their own views on a definitive list of Scriptural books including both the Old and New Testaments.

Another rival theology, the Montanist one we already met, nudged the Church toward consolidating the New Testament in the late II century: the four Gospels and Paul's epistles had achieved wide circulation and largely unquestioned authority within the early Church but hadn't been collected in a single authoritative book yet, so Montanus saw in this fact an

---

314) J. Hannah, *Lecture Notes for the History of Doctrine*, Nav Press, 2002, p.46ff

opportunity to spread his message, by claiming authoritative status for his new revelation. So, Church leaders met the challenge around A.D. 190 and circulated a definitive list of apostolic writings, that is today called the *Muratorian Canon*, after its modern discoverer, which bears striking resemblance to today's New Testament although including two books, *Revelation of Peter* and *Wisdom of Solomon*, which were later excluded from the canon.

By the time of Nicea, but not in the council of Nicea, Church leaders only debated the legitimacy of a few books that we accept today, chief among them *Hebrews* and *Revelation*, because their authorship remained in doubt. In fact, authorship was the most important consideration for those who worked to solidify the canon: early Church leaders considered letters and eyewitness accounts authoritative and binding only if they were written by an apostle or close disciple of an apostle. This way they could be assured of the documents' reliability. Moreover, as pastors and preachers, they also observed which books did in fact build up the Church and saw this as a sign that such books were inspired Scripture. The results , after the mentioned formalization of the canon in Hippo, was the Bible as we know It.[315]

The role of Constantine (who, surely wouldn't have had any preparation, and even interest, in entering a philological and theological discussion of this kind) or of any other emperor in this whole process was absolutely nugatory.

As expressed by Bruce, "*the New Testament books did not become authoritative for the Church because they were formally included in a canonical list; on the contrary, the Church included them in her canon because she already regarded them as divinely inspired, [...]. Councils did not impose something new upon the Christian communities but codified*

---

315) B. M. Metzger, *The Canon of the New Testament: Its Origin, Development, and Significance*, Oxford University Press, 1997, passim

*what was already the general practice of those communities."*³¹⁶ and, under the political point of view, an echo of this idea can be found also in Metzger, who states: *"You have to understand that the canon was not the result of a series of contests involving church politics. [...] . You see, the canon is a list of authoritative books more than it is an authoritative list of books. These documents didn't derive their authority from being selected; each one was authoritative before anyone gathered them together."*³¹⁷

The only relation between Constantine and the canon is given by the fact that, in a letter to the Church historian Eusebius, the emperor did indeed order the preparation of *"fifty copies of the sacred Scriptures."*³¹⁸ But nowhere in the letter does he command that any of the Gospels had to be embellished in order to make Jesus appear more godlike or anything else. And even if he had done so, it would have been virtually impossible to get faithful Christians to accept such accounts.

Consequently, it's also not true that Constantine partook to the choice of which Books were to be included in or excluded from the canon: this process had already been done and it had been based mainly on the cleansing of the canon from any Gnostic writing which did not emphasize the humanity of Jesus, but instead read the gospel message as a spiritual allegory, while also infancy gospels portraying Jesus as a God-child were excluded from the New Testament³¹⁹.

But, if any claim of an imperial participation to the canonic formation and of a discussion about the canon in Nicea sounds

---

316) F.F. Bruce, *The New Testament Documents: Are they reliable?*, IVP, 1960, p.21
317) B. Metzger, interviewed in L.Strobel, *The Case for Christ*, Zondervan, 1998, p.176
318) As remembered already in P. Schaff, *Nicene and Post-Nicene Fathers*, Eerdmans, 1952, p.421
319) L.M. McDonald, *The Formation of the Christian Biblical Canon*, Hendrickson Publishers, 1995, pp. 34-37

only absurd, where does this quite common erroneous idea come from?

Actually it is difficult to find the spring of such a misconception, but, perhaps the root of the diffusion of this thesis could lay in the period of the Enlightenment and in a wrong interpretation by Voltaire, who, in his *Philosophic Dictionary*, wrote:

"The council Fathers distinguished between Scriptural Books and apocryphal books thanks to a quite bizarre expedient: having placed all the books at random on an altar, they considered as apocryphal the ones falling on the ground"[320]

But for a certain taste for the mockery of any form of "religious superstition", typical of the cultural period, it is rather probable, anyway, that Voltaire didn't invent the whole episode on his own. The question was deepened by Hunwick, who, about it, wrote:

"The problem of the distinction between spurious and authentic Gospels was not discussed during the first council of Nicea: the anecdote is totally invented. It appears in the clandestine text La Religion Chretienne Analysée *attributed to Dumarsais and published by Voltaire in abridged form in his* Recueil necessaire *of 1765, where, as a source, he points out the* Sanctissima Concilia *(1671-1672, Paris, vol II, pp 84-85) by Pierre Labbe (1607-1667), affirming to deal with the years 325 § 358 of the* Annales Ecclesiasti *(1559-1607) by Baronius (1538-1607), even if one can see that Baronius, reporting about the adoption of some Gospels and the refusal of others as spurious, doesn't report about the method of the distinction.*

Voltaire repeats the fictional anecdote in several occasions, sometimes mentioning also Labbe as a source (see B. E. Schwarzbach, p. 329 and n. 81). Doubts where previously expressed also by Tillemont (see L. S. Le Nain de Tillemont, Memoires pour servir a l'histoire ecclesiastique, *1701-14, second edition, Paris, Robustel - Arsenal 4°*

---

320) Entry 'Councils', Voltaire, *Philosophic Dictionary*, Paris, 1694 - 1778

H.5547, volume VI, p. 676.)
Actually the anecdote seems to date Baronius six centuries before his birth as it appears initially in an anonymous Synodikon *containing short citations about 158 councils of the first nine centuries. Taaken from Greece in the XVI century by Andreas Darmasius, this document was bought and edited by the Luthern Theologian Johannes Pappus (1549-1610). Later it was reprinted, for sure at least in the* Bibliotheca Graeca *[...] by Fabricius, whose first edition was published in the years 1705-1707, and so, possibly known by D'Holbach. The anecdote can be found in* Synodicon vetus *section 34, "council of Nicaea" (Johannes Albert Fabricius, Biblioteca graeca... [1790-1809, Amburgo: Bohn], Volume XII, pages 370-371.)*"[321]

So, also avoiding to follow the winding track of the reconstruction of the primary source of the mistake, it is, anyway, clear that the whole story comes from a misinterpretation perpetuated along history and having as a final spokesman directly one of the most important philosophers of the Enlightenment.

Anyway, the creation of the canon had nothing to share with a council whose goal, we repeat it once again, was only to grant a unity of the church which was functional to the unity of the whole empire and with an emperor like Constantine, whose worries were merely political and not surely theological.

---

321) Cfr. A. Hunwick, *Critical Edition of Ecce Homo by Baron D'Holbach*, Mouton de Gruyter, 1995, pp. 48-49

Dr. Lawrence M.F. Sudbury – **Nicea: what it was, what it was not**

IV.2) NICEA AFTER NICEA

As anticipated, anyway, the plans of Constantine for a "united Christian Church in a united empire" totally failed, making, in a long term vision, what had to be one of the emperor's greatest successes one of his worst failures.

Although, in fact, the council of Nicea appeared to have succeeded in overthrowing Arianism, it did by no means bring it to an end but merely drove it underground[322]. This was seen only a few months after Nicea, when two leading bishops, Eusebius of Nicomedia and Theognis of Nicea, enlightened the emperor to their dissatisfaction of the creed of A.D. 325 and withdrew their approval of it[323]. Also at this time some of the dispossessed Arians from Alexandria returned to appeal their cause and, obviously, found support in Eusebius and Theognis. As a result, in the orthodox post-Nicene climate of this first years, the appellants were dismissed and the two bishops were sent into exile in Gaul, where they remained for three years, while their former sees were transferred to loyal Nicene adherents[324].

The whole situation change dramatically in A.D. 328, when Constantine had a change of mind over his previous position regarding the Nicene council and allowed the exiled bishops Eusebius and Theognis to return and re-occupy their former sees.

This is probably the most mysterious point of the whole situation: why did Constantine change his mind? Surely he was not convinced by theological considerations and a back track was completely against his plans for unity. Although the exact reasons for the emperor's change are difficult to be clearly

---

322) J.N.D. Kelly, *Early Christian Doctrines*, A&C Black, 1989, p. 237
323) H. Jedin, *History of the Church*, vol. 2, Burns & Oates, 1980, p. 29
324) P. Hughes, *A History of the Church*, vol. 1, Sheed and Ward, 1979, p.193

determined, we don't have to forget that Eusebius of Nicomedia had been for a quite long time the closest bishop to the imperial family: it is, therefore, possible that Constantine's stepsister (Constantia), his mother (Helena) and many other members of the court influenced him to some degree, mainly in consideration to the risk of uprisings of the closest people to him and, perhaps, of the whole town he was living in[325]. In the picture of the need to avoid the presence of any faction putting the imperial authority under discussion, this would have been an even more dangerous problem than the lack of unity inside of the Church.

Whatever the reason, anyway, even Arius himself was called before the emperor for another appraisal of his doctrine. However, the profession of faith that Arius brought before Constantine carefully avoided any mention of the "homoousios" and therefore managed to avoid the primary issues that had been at stake at Nicea and convinced the emperor to acquit him[326]. But despite his new found favor Arius died before he could be reinstated[327].

With the return of the exiled Arians, Eusebius of Nicomedia became a prominent figure in the Arian party[328]. Eusebius was a competent leader who realized that a direct attack on the council of Nicea would fail because of Constantine's attachment to it, so, instead, he turned his attention to discrediting those who were supporters of it (principally

---

325) Jedin, *Cit.*, p.29
326) *Ibid.*, pp. 31-32
327) R. Williams, *Arius Heresy and Tradition*, Longman and Todd, 1987, p. 81. According to Athanasius, it was a Saturday when the Emperor gave the command to Alexander to accept Arius back into Alexandria. As a result of this, Alexander, and a close friend of Athanasius, the presbyter Macarius, prayed in earnest that either he (Alexander) or Arius would die before morning. Subsequently, Arius died from some kind of internal haemorrhage or rupture which Athanasius saw as a judgment from God.
328) Kelly, *Cit.*, p. 237

Eustathius, Marcellus, and Athanasius)[329]. In A.D. 331 Eustathius was the first of Eusebius' opponents to be deposed and this was further reinforced by Constantine, who issued a second sentence of exile: the main charge, that of heresy, originated in Eustathius' emphasis of God's unity which led to accusations of Sabellianism[330].

Eusebius' main opponent was Athanasius who had taken over the Alexandrian see after the death of Alexander in A.D. 328. Athanasius, who followed the same theological convictions of Alexander, soon became known as the great champion of the Nicene faith, but opposition emerged against him in A.D. 335, at Tyre, when he was brought before a council dominated by the Arian party. Although he had arrived with forty-nine bishops from Egypt who professed the faith of Nicea, they were not permitted to enter[331]. It was on account of such discrimination that Athanasius appealed directly to the emperor himself and appealed for justice. Contantine's solution was to call for the synod to re-assemble before him at Constantinople; but only four, the two Eusebiuses, Ursacius, and Valens, complied with the emperor's wishes[332]. The four men brought a new charge against Athanasius by accusing him of scheming to hinder the capitals supply of corn, which resulted in his prompt exile by the Emperor to distant Treves and Moselle[333]. Marcellus of Ancyra was also condemned at a synod in Constantinople in A.D. 336 for holding to Sabellian beliefs: however, it appears that there was some substance to this particular charge which is

---

329) J.L. Gonzalez, *A History of Christian Thought*, vol. 1, Abingdon Press, 1970, 281
330) *Ibid.*, pp. 281-282. Other reasons for his condemnation included accusations of speaking disrespectfully of Constantine's mother and charges of adultery
331) Hughes, *Cit.*, p. 194
332) Jedin, *Cit.*, p.31
333) Hughes, *Cit.*, p.199

reflected in Athanasius' attack on his doctrines in one of his works[334].

Just prior to his death in A.D. 337, Constantine, influenced by the Arian party, was as already mentioned, baptised as an Arian by Eusebius and, after his death Constantine's three sons, ruled the empire: Constantine II and Constans shared their rulership in the West while Constantius became Emperor of the East[335].

Although the exiles were permitted to return, it soon became cleart that the new political situation in the East favoured the Arian Christology. However, Arianism had never really managed to flourish as successfully in the West because there was less fear of Sabellianism, and the formula "One God in three Persons" was common and in harmony with the Nicene Christological thinking. Political unrest emerged in the West between the two emperors and continued until the death of Constantine II in A.D. 340. Despite a further exile to Rome in A.D. 339 Athanasius was eventually allowed to return to Alexandria in A.D. 346 when Constantius became more moderate in his Arian convictions due to the influence of Constans[336].

From the death of Constans in A.D. 350, Constantius reigned as sole emperor and through him a determined effort was made by his Arian advisors to bypass the Nicene doctrine with a formula that proclaimed the Son to be clearly subordinate to the Father (the so-called "Blasphemy of Sirmium", dated A.D. 357)[337]. For them, the Son was unlike the Father in all things, and of a different substance[338]. They argued that while He could be called God in a sense, this was merely used to describe His connection and activity with the Father. But unlike Arius

---

334) Gonzales, *Cit.*, pp.283-284
335) Jedin, *Cit.*, p.33
336) Gonzales, *Cit.*, p.285
337) Kelly, *Cit.*, p. 238
338) *Ibid.* p. 249

they believed that the Son did possess a form of divinity insofar as he was active in creation[339].

This section of the anti-Nicene party, who were to become known as "Anomoeans", or extreme Arians, succeeded in getting their thoroughly subordinationist creed established in the East, and was enforced violently in the West. Part of the formula that they proposed is as follows: *"For it can be doubtful to none that the Father is greater than the Son in honour, dignity, splendour majesty, and in the very name of the Father, the Son Himself testifying 'He who sent me is greater than I.'"*. The creed also goes on to say that the Son is *"subordinated to the Father."*[340]

Although it appeared that the Arians were victorious, many showed themselves to be dissatisfied. Many of those who had previously followed Eusebius of Nicomedia's Arianism, and rejected Nicea, had done so not because of a true Arian conviction but mainly because they had suspected the "Nicean creed" of being a form of Sabellianism. But with the "Blasphemy of Sirmium", the most moderate theologians reacted strongly against the Anomoeans' attack on the Son's divinity[341]. These reactions appeared in Gaul, North Africa, and amongst the most moderate Arian circles in the East. Many of these Eastern bishops held to a high Christology and had been influenced by Origen's eternal generation of the Son; it was only the Nicene use of the term "homoousios" that they found unacceptable[342].

The "Homoeans" (also called "political Arians") emerged and reasoned that the Son was *"like the Father in all things"* (although they later asserted that the Son was simply *"like the Father"*)[343]. Some in this group, such as Ursacius and Valens were extreme

---

339) Gonzales, *Cit.*, p.285
340) J.N.D. Kelly, *Early Christian Creeds*, Longman Group Ltd., 1972, p. 286
341) Jedin, *Cit.*, p.46
342) W.H.C. Frend, *The Early Church*, Fortress Press, 1985, p. 147
343) Gonzales, *Cit.*, p.288

Arians who supported the "Anomoean" agenda when they could, but generally tended to avoid any discussion on the subject of the "homoousios" so that they would not have to define what they really meant by their statement *"like the Father"*[344]. Others in the "Homoean party" objected strongly to the "Anomoean" statements about the Son and declared Him to be born of the substance ("ousia") of the Father, but, at the same time, they refused to acknowledge Him as true Deity[345]. Basil of Ancyra emerged as the leader of the group who became known as "Homoiousians" when in A.D. 358 he gathered together a synod and proposed the term "homoiousios" to describe the Son as being of "like substance" to the Father including His essential being ("ousia")[346]. With this proposal, the "Homoiousians" affirmed that the Son is to be considered next to the Father, not as a mere created being, but, at the same time, they avoided being misunderstood as Sabellians because they stressed a distinction between the Father and the Son[347].

This managed to win the approval of the Emperor from the "Anomoeans". Although the "Homoiousians" were initially opposed to both the Arians and the Nicene party, their new term undoubtedly meant a significant move towards the view of Nicea[348].

Constantius, seeking reconciliation between the anti-Nicene groups called twin councils at Arminium and Seleucia in A.D. 359. At these councils the term "ousia" was rejected and it was argued that although both "homoousios" and "homoiousios" had no Scriptural warrant, the term "homoios" did, and meant

---

344) *Ibid.*
345) J.H. Newman, *The Arians of the Fourth Century*, Longmans Green and Co., 1909, p. 298
346) T. Dowley, *The History of Christianity*, Lion Publishing, 1990, p. 172
347) Gonzales, *Cit.*, p.290
348) Jedin, *Cit.*, p.46

the same as "homoiousios". By A.D. 360, bishops in both East and West had completely rejected the term "homoousios" as being unscriptural. This was the situation which instigated Jerome to write, *"The whole world groaned and marveled to find itself Arian"*[349].

With the death of Constantius, Julian the Apostate permitted all exiles to return and work out any differences, theologically rather than politically[350]. With this opportunity Athanasius gathered a synod in Alexandria in A.D. 362 and, to the surprise of Julian, there was mutual understanding between the various groups. The synod was a great success for Athanasius, although he was exiled again by Julian for a brief period afterwards[351].

Gonzalez observes how the Christological issue of the synod of Alexandria also opened discussions regarding the Spirit. Although the majority of bishops had by this time accepted the divinity of the Son in one way or another, there were some among their ranks who insisted that the Spirit was not coequal with the Father and the Son. Those who held to this position were called "Pneumatomachians" (enemies of the Spirit) and were condemned along with Arianism. Therefore, by condemning both Arianism and Pneumatomachianism, an alliance was strengthened between the Nicenes and the conservative "Homoiousians" and the first steps towards Trinitarianism was affirmed. But despite the new relationships formed between the two groups, clarifications of terms were still needed, especially regarding the use of the words "homoousios", "ousia" and "hypostasis" and how they applied

---

349) Frend, *Cit.*, pp. 156-157
350) Newman, *Cit.*, p. 354. Newman notes how Julian, being well aware of the various differences amongst the Christians, had hoped for a spectacular conflict. It was even said that he had invited the leaders of the different groups to his own palace *"that he might enjoy the agreeable spectacle of their furious encounters"*.
351) Dowley, *Cit.*, pp.173-174

to the Godhead[352].

Clearer explanation developed with the coming of three theologians, Gregory of Nazianzus and two brothers, Basil of Caesarea and Gregory of Nyssa, who were to become known as the "Cappadocian Fathers"[353]. Their primary concern focused on the terms "ousia" and "hypostasis", and how they had to be understood as being distinct rather than synonymous as was commonly thought. The Cappadocian theologians interpreted "hypostasis" as an individual subsistence and "ousia" as the common essence, and went on to argue that in the Godhead there existed three "hypostases" and one "ousia". Consequently, with the acceptance of these terms by those in the West, and eventually the East, the Cappadocians were also able to demonstrate the faithfulness of the Christological term "homoousios"[354].

In the confusion and misunderstanding of terms since the council of Nicea, up to the success of the Cappadocians, another controversy of a different kind had also emerged. Apollinarius, bishop of Laodicea, had raised the question of how the humanity and Deity were united in the one Person of Jesus Christ: Apollinarius propagated the teaching that the "Logos" took the place of the human soul in Christ which led to the belief that Christ did not possess a full human nature and that He was incapable of experiencing any real human emotions[355].

"Apollinarianism", along with all of the various Arian and Arianizing deviations that had inflicted the Church for so long were soon to be placed under a ban and the faith of Nicea was to be accepted once again.

---

352) Gonzales, *Cit.*, pp. 291-294.
353) F.J.F. Jackson, *The History of the Christian Church to A.D. 461*, George Allen and Unwin Ltd., 1965, p.380
354) Gonzales, *Cit.*, pp. 294-295
355) Jackson, *Cit.*, p.391

Kelly notes how the final overthrow of Arianism started only with the rule of Julian (quite paradoxically, being this emperor such a convinced pagan to pass to history with the nickname of "the Apostate") in A.D.361, up to the council of Constantinople in A.D. 381[356].

After the death of Julian in A.D. 363 up to the acceptance of Nicea under Theodosius in A.D. 381, there emerged a long succession of emperors who were either in favor of the Nicene party or at the least did not support the Arians.

Under the Emperor Theodosius, a firm attempt was made to try to do what Nicea had completely failed in doing, that's to say, to bring unity once more to the empire: this attempt was brought on with the calling of the council of Constantinople in A.D. 381. Being of a traditional Western bias, Theodosius urged that the faith of Nicea should be accepted by all his subjects and it was the Cappadocian formula that managed to prepare the way for the acceptance and reaffirmation of Nicea, while "Pneumatomachianism" and "Apollinarianism" were excluded as unorthodox heresies[357].

Although after the council of Nicea Arianism had continued to grow, actually it was inevitable that its apparent success as a Christological doctrine would be short lived: every time the Arians expressed their doctrine in its most extreme form, the Christian conscience would react strongly against what was regarded to be an attack on the true honor that was due to Christ. So the faith of the Nicene party, although in a sense it wasless rational than that of the Arians and although it took more than half a century to define clearly its true meaning, was finally able to reaffirm its rightful place, but what we need to observe and underline is that, although the final creed of the Christian Church became the one of Nicea (an, actually, even

---

356) J.N.D. Kelly, *Early Christian Doctrines*, A&C Black, 1989, p. 288
357) Gonzales, *Cit.*, pp. 295-296

with some modifications), finally the unity of the Church was not a product of Nicea, which, in the end, completely failed in its task, but of later councils, nor it was an element to be ascribed in any sense to Constantine, who didn't succeed neither in forming a compact Christian party to support his reign, nor in keeping the empire united after his death and, furthermore, was probably, with his change of mind in A.D. 328, the principal cause of the need of forty more years of discussions and harsh fightings to obtain a Christological unity in Christian doctrines.

IV.3) CONCLUSIONS: QUESTIONS AND ANSWERS

At the beginning of the present study, the goal was to try to understand which of the elements commonly attributed to the council of Nicea could be considered historically true.

By an extensive research related to the social and political background of the council, to the situation of the Church before, during and after the council and to the chronicles and documents produced about and by the council itself, it has been possible to gather a quite large amount of information, which can allow us to have a more precise vision of the events under examination.

In this picture, possibly the best way to conclude this essay is to formulate once again all the most important questions which can be referred to the council of Nicea and to give them an answer on the base of the collected elements, in a classical "Question and Answer scheme".

Q: Which were the meaning and the goal of the council of Nicea for the Church?

A: Theoretically, the meaning of the council was to re-establish a unity in the Christian theology and liturgical praxis and the goal was to eradicate any form of heresy and in particular the Arian one, which was spreading from Egypt, putting orthodoxy in crisis.

Practically, things can be seen in a quite different way. Arianism was just one of the many Christological heresies having birth in the last one hundred years before the council and, probably not even the most dangerous one: Sabellianism, Montanism and the Marcion's heresy were possibly even more disrupting for the orthodoxy. In the end, the idea of establishing a sort of hierarchy inside of the Trinity, although heretic, was much less disruptive than considering Jesus Christ a simple man or than creating two different arrays between "good" and "bad" bishops.

So, one can wonder why it was felt the need to organize a general ecumenic council to solve a fundamentally localized (as related more or less only to some areas of the Eastern Church) problem, already condemned in two previous meetings, when in all similar circumstances local decision had been considered enough.

It is quite clear the all the other items discussed in Nicea were simply complementary to this main item and, but for the date of Easter, whose problem had been already solved in the majority of dioceses, they were all of lesser importance and could be managed in more local ways (and actually, although called ecumenic, the council of Nicea was, in spite of the presence of so many bishops, a quite partial council, with a large presence of the Eastern Church and an almost symbolic presence of the Western one).

Clearly stated that none of the subjects mentioned by recent publications, such as the question of the canon, which was not even touched at large, or the problem of the divinity of Christ, which, although discussed in relation to its nature, was never doubted by anyone (but for a minoritarian group of the most extremist Arians), unlike it happened, in example, in other heresies as the Ebionite one or the Sabellianism, it looks like the whole matter pivoted only on the Arian dispute.

Paradoxically, to give such an enormous prominence to the heresy of Arius, instead of solving it, focused the attention of the whole Church on his thesis, spreading them and radicalizing the positions of the two arrays.

The question, therefore, remains: why to call an ecumenic council?

Probably the answer can be found only looking back to the position of a Church just coming out from one of the harshest persecutions of its history and, for the first time, having the possibility to obtain an imperial patronage by Constantine.

Obviously, the Church had to give something in exchange and this "something" was to condescend to the will of the emperor, whose goals were absolutely not theological.

Q: Which were the meaning and the goal of the council of Nicea for Constantine?

A: We spoke about the reasons of Constantine all along the text, but, here, we can try to summarize them in some main points. The period in which Constantine achieved his crown was a troubled one: he was the first emperor to govern alone after the beginning of the tetrarchy with Diocletian and in the hundred years before him, just a few emperors had had a natural death. Moreover, also personally, he hadn't been the best pretender to the throne, being, actually, only the illegitimate child of the caesar Constans and he had obtained the supremacy thanks to his military capabilities, to the inadequacy of his rivals and to the faithfulness of his legions.

This last element must not be underestimated. For a very long period, possibly with the only exception of Diocletian, the emperors had been something like puppets of the army and the army, in which the same cult professed by Constantine, the one of the Unconquered Sun, was still prevalent, was more and more subjected to an "infiltration" of the Christian worshiping.

Also the situation of the empire in the moment of the rise to power of the emperor was not exactly flourish: long years of civil war, an economy progressively in decadence, a bureaucratic system unable to manage an enormous territorial extension and therefore becoming more and more locally autonomous, the continuous dangers at the borders and the drive towards independence of many areas were making its internal cohesion very fragile.

This is the central point of the question: Constantine needed a new glue to keep the empire united and integrated and Christianity looked, in that specific moment, like being an excellent glue.

Christianity, although not being the majority religion of the empire yet, was a power in spectacular growth due to its salvation message appealing to all classes. Furthermore, it was a quite organized and hierarchic body which, being based on the cult and on a sort of mastery tradition, assured the obedience of its believers.

Therefore, to have Christianity on his side seemed to Constantine the best choice to obtain his goals of a stronger imperial unity and of a strengthening of his personal power: this is the main reason of his choice of establishing a "do ut des" policy towards the Christian Church. The "do" side of the agreement included the recognition of a favored position to Christianity in the vast panorama of the many religions of the empire, with privileges going from the help in building new churches to many fiscal and social helps. The "des" side was, on the other hand, the recognition by the Church of his patronage and, in some ways, also of his role of political leadership in the direction of the secular matters of the Church body.

Here we reach the clue point of all the question. We already spoke about the need of Constantine to have a united and homogeneous allied, without internal divisions and factions which could weaken its role of adhesive element as planned by the emperor. But Nicea was not only a possibility to re-establish (or just establish) a monolithic Church unity, which, in any case, with the continuous insurgence of new theological currents related to the uncertain Christology of a young cult still in development, seemed to be everything but probable. Nicea was also, if not mainly, a way for the emperor to show to the whole world the new situation of relations between himself and the Church, a situation in which his patronage had to be evident for everybody, both in terms of new friendship between himself and the Christianity and in terms of decisional (caesaropapistic) power about all the matters related to the secular life of the Church itself, as we can see by the tone and style of some of his letters. Notably, this new status had to be clear, first of all, to all the bishops leading the different local communities: they had to be accomplished both of the imperial goodwill in helping them restoring the orthodoxy and of the power of the emperor in, eventually, repressing any attempt to react to the new situation. From here, the need of an ecumenical council, able both to show and to ratify the position of Constantine towards Christianity, the idea to move it from Ancyra (where local machinations could darken the show of its total control) to Nicea, a place in which, in the imperial palaces, he could display all his grandeur, and the attempt of the emperor (actually quite frustrated by the scarce attendance from the Western dioceses) to have an as large as possible presence of bishops in occasion of a synod whose occasion (and, somehow, we could even speak about a pretext) was a dispute that, it must be said once more, was not harder than many others before.

Q: Which was the role of Constantine in the development of the council?

A: Accordingly, the role of Constantine in the whole council was simply the one of a powerful and magnificent amphitryon moving, through his presence and mainly through the presidency of Hosius, all the elements so to achieve his two goals mentioned above (unity of a precious allied and display of the new "state of the arts" towards the leaders of the Church). His role was, therefore, simply political and absolutely not theological. We have to remember the total indifference of the emperor for any thin theological and Christological distinction: perhaps he was a Christian (in the sense that, mixing and confusing the figures of the Unconquered Sun and of Jesus Christ he could also be considered, in a very personal and deviant way, a sort of believer) but surely he was not an orthodox Catholic (neither in terms of deep beliefs nor in terms of life-style). Moreover, very possibly, in his quite sketchy knowledge of the Christian theology, proved by his waving attitude towards the Orthodoxes and the Arians, he was unable or uninterested to understand the different Christological approaches of the two arrays: the choice between Hosius or Eusebius of Nicomedia was, for him, only political, dictated by the moment and by the party which could best accomplish the task to help him in reaching his goals.

Any idea of an imperial personal involvement in the definition of a theological line or in the choice of a determined Christological theory is absolutely improper, as well as it is improper to think about any correlation between Constantine and the elaboration of a canon: all this elements were not inside of the sphere of interest of the emperor, who saw the Church mainly as a useful tool to accomplish his goals and the synod as a great stage to perform his new role of political patron (and somehow leader) of the expanding Christianity.

Q: Which were the most important elements emerging in the council?

A: In the line of what said before, probably the most important elements emerging during the council of Nicea were, but for the obvious condemnation of Arianism and resolution of minor disputes like the Easter related one, the weight of the imperial presence in the decisions and, although often underestimated, the role assigned to the church of Jerusalem by the council Fathers.

In relation to the first item, we must identify ourselves with the situation of the bishops: the supreme authority of the most powerful empire of history is present to any seat of the council, held, not without a sense, in a quite Arian town in which the only warranty of impartiality in the development of the works is theoretically given only by the imposing display of power of the emperor, in form of a huge security corp. The whole "set design" is, by the way, meant just to impose the presence and importance of the imperial commitment to the synod: Constantine, in every moment, since his opening of the sessions to his final banquet, puts himself in the center of the scene. We don't have to be cheated by the apparent understatement which comes out from the words of the emperor: he is not a simple spectator of the council, but, actually, the main character of it, although acting through a sort of body double represented by Hosius. This doesn't mean that Hosius was only a spokesman of Constantine: he was the leader of the party chosen by the emperor (probably against all the expectations of the Arians) to play his game in that determined occasion and it's quite fundamental that practically the whole council ends with his proposal and with the ratification of it by Constantine. Since that moment on, there is no more room for a real discussion as the emperor has expressed, indirectly and then directly his will: the council, once again, clearly shows to be what it effectively was, that's to say a political event under the pretext of a theological synod.

The second element, the only alluded new power attributed to the Jerusalem see, can, at first sight, seem to be a bit dissonant with the whole context of the council: in a synod organized to give unity back to the Church, the idea to partially balance the power of Rome with a second power in the East looks like being rather absurd. But, if we pay attention to the context and see the whole meeting under the different light of an imperial power display, we can easily realize that this decision is perfectly consequent. If the will of Constantine was, in fact, to establish himself as a sort of secondary, temporal authority inside of the Church, beside the one of the bishop of Rome, the creation of a second center of power was symbolically coherent with this decision in stating a first degree of separation from the concept of a unique central power and, with the pretext of asserting the historical importance of the see of Jerusalem, in creating a nucleus of power that didn't only satisfy the will of stronger independence of the Eastern bishops, but, being close to the area of Constantine's strict control, could be more easily influenced by him, although not being so openly a new center of alternative power as it would have been in case the bishops had granted the same level of honor to Nicomedia or Constantinople (which, perhaps, wouldn't have been so easily accepted by the whole Church).

Q: Which were the results of the council? Was the council successful in reaching its goals?

A: Once stated that the council of Nicea was meant to be not only a ecclesiastic but also a political event, we must naturally speak about two different orders of results: the theological and the political ones. In both cases, anyway, the success of Nicea can be evaluated in different ways if we analyze it in the short, medium or long term.

Theologically, the synod was, obviously, successful in the very short term, with the theoretical condemnation and elimination of the Arian heresy, the homogenization of many liturgical issues, the clarification and emanation of some legislative elements and, mainly, with the redaction of the Nicene creed, which, although being still quite vague in its main lines and, in the attempt to be a kind of syncretic mean to satisfy all parties, finally satisfied none, was meant to be the perpetual seal of the Catholic faith. This was, anyway, simply a success due not to an agreement of the parts but to the imposition of a line, we must repeat it once again, supported by the theoretically external imperial power, on another line. The victory of the "homousians" was, therefore, just a pyrrhic victory as, instead of creating a unity in the Church Christology, it further splayed the positions, ending by becoming, as seen, a spring for new conflicts. Even the creed, although accepted by a wide majority in its final Nicean redaction, had later, in the council of Constantinople of A.D. 381, to be quite largely reformulated[358]

---

358) A comparison of the two texts shows the rather deep differences between the two creeds. The creed of Nicea sounds like: *"We believe in*

to adapt to a real orthodox Christology, not keeping into account the polemical attacks towards other heretic factions. What we can say is that, probably, the council of Nicea was successful only in drawing some rough sketches of a long term plan for a future orthodoxy or, even more, to focus the attention of the Church on the need to look for a Christological and organizational unity. In this sense, on the theological point of view, the whole synod was just a little more than a mere declaration of statements.

Partially different was the situation in relation to the political

---

one God the Father All-sovereign, maker of all things. And in one Lord Jesus Christ, the Son of God, begotten of the Father, only-begotten, that is, of the substance of the Father, God of God, Light of Light, true God of true God, begotten not made, of one substance with the Father, through whom all things were made, things in heaven and things on the earth; who for us men and for our salvation came down and was made flesh, and became man, suffered, and rose on the third day, ascended into the heavens, and is coming to judge living and dead. And in the Holy Spirit. And those that say 'There was when he was not,' and, 'Before he was begotten he was not,' and that, 'He came into being from what-is-not,' or those that allege, that the son of God is 'Of another substance or essence' or 'created,' or 'changeable' or 'alterable,' these the Catholic and Apostolic Church anathematizes.", while the one of Constantinople, obviously deriving from the previous one, is: *"We believe in one God, the Father, the Almighty, maker of heaven and earth, of all that is, seen and unseen. We believe in one Lord, Jesus Christ, the only Son of God, eternally begotten of the Father, God from God, Light from Light, true God from true God, begotten, not made, of one Being with the Father. Through him all things were made. For us and for our salvation he came down from heaven. By the power of the Holy Spirit he became incarnate from the Virgin Mary, and was made man. For our sake he was crucified under Pontius Pilate, he suffered death and was buried. On the third day he rose again in accordance with the Scriptures. He ascended in heaven and is seated at the right hand of the Father. He will come again in glory to judge the living and the dead, and his kingdom will have no end. We believe in the Holy Spirit, the Lord, the giver of life, who proceeds from the Father [and the Son]. With the Father and the Son he is worshiped and glorified. He has spoken through the Prophets. We believe in one holy catholic and apostolic Church. We acknowledge one baptism for the forgiveness of sins. We look for the resurrection of the dead, and the life of the world to come. Amen."*

results of the council. Again, we can speak about an initial success reached by Constantine in obtaining a sort of imposed unity in the ranks of his chosen allied and in fully displaying his role of patron. What happens after A.D. 328 is still quite mysterious, with his sudden volte-face in favor of the Arians, probably due to circumstances beyond his control and to higher political needs. Surely, this sudden change of his mind can be seen as one of the most important causes of the failure of the imperial policy for the unity of the Church in the medium term. But it is in relation to the second goal, the establishment of a sort of perpetual imperial patronage on the Christian Church and the creation of a link between the spiritual power and the secular one that the policy of Constantine managed to succeed also in the long term: the linkage officially expressed for the first time in Nicea and the trend of an active involvement of the imperial power, often at the border of caesaropapism if not directly definable in this terms, in the spiritual decisions of the Church became, with the short exception of the period of the emperor Julian, a constitutive element of the whole period of the late empire and of the high Middle Ages, becoming, not surprisingly, the most long-lasting result of a synod whose meaning was, basically, since its very first call, markedly politically addressed towards this direction.

APPENDIX I:
THE CAPTIONS OF THE ARABIC CANONS ATTRIBUTED TO THE COUNCIL OF NICEA

- Canon I.- Insane persons and energumens should not be ordained.
- Canon II. - Bond servants are not to be ordained.
- Canon III. - Neophytes in the faith are not to be ordained to Holy Orders before they have a knowledge of Holy Scripture. And such, if convicted after their ordination of grave sin, are to be deposed with those who ordained them.
- Canon IV. - The cohabitation of women with bishops, presbyters, and deacons prohibited on account of their celibacy. We decree that bishops shall not live with women; nor shall a presbyter who is a widower; neither shall they escort them; nor be familiar with them, nor gaze upon them persistently. And the same decree is made with regard to every celibate priest, and the same concerning such deacons as have no wives. And this is to be the case whether the woman be beautiful or ugly, whether a young girl or beyond the age of puberty, whether great in birth, or an orphan taken out of charity under pretext of bringing her up. For the devil with such arms slays religious, bishops, presbyters, and deacons, and incites them to the fires of desire. But if she be an old woman, and of advanced age, or a sister, or mother, or aunt, or grandmother, it is permitted to live with these because such persons are free from all suspicion of scandal.
- Canon V. - Of the election of a bishop and of the confirmation of the election.
- Canon VI. - That those excommunicated by one bishop are not to be received by another; and that those whose excommunication has been shown to have been unjust should be absolved by the archbishop or patriarch.
- Canon VII. - That provincial Councils should be held twice a year, for the consideration of all things affecting the churches of the bishops of the province.
- Canon VIII. - Of the patriarchs of Alexandria and Antioch, and of their jurisdiction.
- Canon IX. - Of one who solicits the episcopate when the people do not wish him; or if they do desire him, but without the consent of the archbishop.

- Canon X. - How the bishop of Jerusalem is to be honored, the honor, however, of the metropolitan church of Cæsarea being preserved intact, to which he is subject.
- Canon XI. - Of those who force themselves into the order of presbyters without election or examination.
- Canon XII. - Of the bishop who ordains one whom he understands has denied the faith; also of one ordained who after that he had denied it, crept into orders.
- Canon XIII. - Of one who of his own will goes to another church, having been chosen by it, and does not wish afterwards to stay there. Of taking pains that he be transferred from his own church to another.
- Canon XIV. - No one shall become a monk without the bishop's license, and why a license is required.
- Canon XV. - That clerics or religious who lend on usury should be cast from their grade.
- Canon XVI. - Of the honour to be paid to the bishop and to a presbyter by the deacons.
- Canon XVII. - Of the system and of the manner of receiving those who are converted from the heresy of Paul of Samosata.
- Canon XVIII. - Of the system and manner of receiving those who are converted from the heresy the Novatians.
- Canon XIX. - Of the system and manner of receiving those who return after a lapse from the faith, and of receiving the relapsed, and of those brought into peril of death by sickness before their penance is finished, and concerning such as are convalescent.
- Canon XX. - Of avoiding the conversation of evil workers and wizards, also of the penance of them that have not avoided such.
- Canon XXI. - Of incestuous marriages contrary to the law of spiritual relationship, and of the penance of such as are in such marriages.
- Canon XXII. - Of sponsors in baptism. Men shall not hold females at the font, neither women males; but women females, and men males.
- Canon XXIII. - Of the prohibited marriages of spiritual brothers and sisters from receiving them in baptism.
- Canon XXIV. - Of him who has married two wives at the same time, or who through lust has added another woman to his wife; and of his punishment.
- Canon XXV. - That no one should be forbidden Holy Communion

unless such as are doing penance.
- Canon XXVI. - Clerics are forbidden from suretyship or witness-giving in criminal causes.
- Canon XXVII. - Of avoiding the excommunicate, and of not receiving the oblation from them; and of the excommunication of him who does not avoid the excommunicated.
- Canon XXVIII. - How anger, indignation, and hatred should be avoided by the priest, especially because he has the power of excommunicating others.
- Canon XXIX. - Of not kneeling in prayer.
- Canon XXX. - Of giving names of Christians in baptism, and of heretics who retain the faith in the Trinity and the perfect form of baptism; and of others not retaining it, worthy of a worse name, and of how such are to be received when they come to the faith.
- Canon XXXI. - Of the system and manner of receiving converts to the Orthodox faith from the heresy of Arius and of other like.
- Canon XXXII. - Of the system of receiving those who have kept the dogmas of the faith and the Church's laws, and yet have separated from us and afterwards come back.
- Canon XXXIII. - Of the place of residence of the Patriarch, and of the honour which should be given to the bishop of Jerusalem and to the bishop of Seleucia.
- Canon XXXIV. - Of the honour to be given to the Archbishop of Seleucia in the Synod of Greece.
- Canon XXXV. - Of not holding a provincial synod in the province of Persia without the authority of the patriarch of Antioch, and how the bishops of Persia are subject to the metropolitans of Antioch.
- Canon XXXVI. - Of the creation of a patriarch for Ethiopia, and of his power, and of the honour to be paid him in the Synod of Greece.
- Canon XXXVII. - Of the election of the Archbishop of Cyprus, who is subject to the patriarch of Antioch.
- Canon XXXVIII. - That the ordination of ministers of the Church by bishops in the dioceses of strangers is forbidden.
- Canon XXXIX. - Of the care and power which a Patriarch has over the bishops and archbishops of his patriarchate; and of the primacy of the Bishop of Rome over all. Let the patriarch consider what things are done by the archbishops and bishops in their provinces; and if he shall find anything done by them otherwise

than it should be, let him change it, and order it, as seemeth him fit: for he is the father of all, and they are his sons. And although the archbishop be among the bishops as an elder brother, who hath the care of his brethren, and to whom they owe obedience because he is over them; yet the patriarch is to all those who are under his power, just as he who holds the seat of Rome, is the head and prince of all patriarchs; inasmuch as he is first, as was Peter, to whom power is given over all Christian princes, and over all their peoples, as he who is the Vicar of Christ our Lord over all peoples and over the whole Christian Church, and whoever shall contradict this, is excommunicated by the Synod. Let there be only four patriarchs in the whole world as there are four writers of the Gospel, and four rivers, etc. And let there be a prince and chief over them, the lord of the see of the Divine Peter at Rome, according as the Apostles commanded. And after him the lord of the great Alexandria, which is the see of Mark. And the third is the lord of Ephesus, which is the see of John the Divine who speaks divine things. And the fourth and last is my lord of Antioch, which is another see of Peter. And let all the bishops be divided under the hands of these four patriarchs; and the bishops of the little towns which are under the dominion of the great cities let them be under the authority of these metropolitans. But let every metropolitan of these great cities appoint the bishops of his province, but let none of the bishops appoint him, for he is greater than they. Therefore let every man know his own rank, and let him not usurp the rank of another. And whosoever shall contradict this law which we have established the Fathers of the Synod subject him to anathema.

- Canon XL. - Of the provincial synod which should be held twice every year, and of its utility; together with the excommunication of such as oppose the decree.
- Canon XLI. - Of the synod of Archbishops, which meets once a year with the Patriarch, and of its utility; also of the collection to be made for the support of the patriarch throughout the provinces and places subject to the patriarch.
- Canon XLII. - Of a cleric or monk who when fallen into sin, and summoned once, twice, and thrice, does not present himself for trial.
- Canon XLIII. - What the patriarch should do in the case of a defendant set at liberty unpunished by the decision of the bishop, presbyter, or even of a deacon, as the case may be.

- Canon XLIV. - How an archbishop ought to give trial to one of his suffragan bishops.
- Canon XLV. - Of the receiving of complaints and condemnation of an archbishop against his patriarch.
- Canon XLVI. - How a patriarch should admit a complaint; or judgment of an Archbishop against an Archbishop.
- Canon XLVII. - Of those excommunicated by a certain one, when they can be and when they cannot be absolved by another.
- Canon XLVIII. - No bishop shall choose his own successor.
- Canon XLIX. - No simoniacal ordinations shall be made.
- Canon L. - There shall be but one bishop of one city, and one parochus of one town; also the incumbent, whether bishop or parish priest, shall not be removed in favour of a successor desired by some of the people unless he has been convicted of manifest crime.
- Canon LI. - Bishops shall not allow the separation of a wife from her husband on account of discord
- Canon LII. - Usury and the base seeking of worldly gain is forbidden to the clergy, also conversation and fellowship with Jews.
- Canon LIII. - Marriages with infidels to be avoided.
- Canon LIV. - Of the election of a chorepiscopus, and of his duties in towns, and villages, and monasteries.
- Canon LV. - How a chorepiscopus should visit the churches and monasteries which are under his jurisdiction.
- Canon LVI. - Of how the presbyters of the towns and villages should go twice a year with their chorepiscopus to salute the bishop, and how religious should do so once a year from their monasteries, and how the new abbot of a monastery should go thrice.
- Canon LVII. - Of the rank in sitting during the celebration of service in church by the bishop, the archdeacon and the chorepiscopus; and of the office of archdeacon, and of the honour due the archpresbyter.
- Canon LVIII. - Of the honour due the archdeacon and the chorepiscopus when they sit in church during the absence of the bishop, and when they go about with the bishop.
- Canon LIX. - How all the grades of the clergy and their duties should be publicly described and set forth.
- Canon LX. - Of how men are to be chosen from the diocese for holy orders, and of how they should be examined.

- Canon LXI. - Of the honour due to the deacons, and how the clerics must not put themselves in their way.
- Canon LXII. - The number of presbyters and deacons is to be adapted to the work of the church and to its means.
- Canon LXIII. - Of the Ecclesiastical Economist and of the others who with him care for the church's possessions.
- Canon LXIV. - Of the offices said in the church, the night and day offices, and of the collect for all those who rule that church.
- Canon LXV. - Of the order to be observed at the funeral of a bishop, of a chorepiscopus and of an archdeacon, and of the office of exequies.
- Canon LXVI. - Of taking a second wife, after the former one has been disowned for any cause, or even not put away, and of him who falsely accuses his wife of adultery. If any priest or deacon shall put away his wife on account of her fornication, or for other cause, as aforesaid, or cast her out of doors for external good, or that he may change her for another more beautiful, or better, or richer, or does so out of his lust which is displeasing to God; and after she has been put away for any of these causes he shall contract matrimony with another, or without having put her away shall take another, whether free or bond; and shall have both equally, they living separately and he sleeping every night with one or other of them, or else keeping both in the same house and bed, let him be deposed. If he were a layman let him be deprived of communion. But if anyone falsely defames his wife charging her with adultery, so that he turns her out of doors, the matter must be diligently examined; and if the accusation was false, he shall be deposed if a cleric, but if a layman shall be prohibited from entering the church and from the communion of the faithful; and shall be compelled to live with her whom he has defamed, even though she be deformed, and poor, and insane; and whoever shall not obey is excommunicated by the Synod. Whatever presbyter or deacon shall put away his wife without the offence of fornication, or for any other cause of which we have spoken above, and shall cast her out of doors…such a person shall be cast out of the clergy, if he were a clergyman; if a layman he shall be forbidden the communion of the faithful….But if that woman [untruly charged by her husband with adultery], that is to say his wife, spurns his society on account of the injury he has done her and the charge he has brought against her, of which she is innocent, let her freely be

put away and let a bill of repudiation be written for her, noting the false accusation which had been brought against her. And then if she should wish to marry some other faithful man, it is right for her to do so, nor does the Church forbid it; and the same permission extends as well to men as to women, since there is equal reason for it for each. But if he shall return to better fruit which is of the same kind, and shall conciliate to himself the love and benevolence of his consort, and shall be willing to return to his pristine friendship, his fault shall be condoned to him after he has done suitable and sufficient penance. And whoever shall speak against this decree the fathers of the synod excommunicate him.

- Canon LXVII. - Of having two wives at the same time, and of a woman who is one of the faithful marrying an infidel; and of the form of receiving her to penance.
- Canon LXVIII. - Of giving in marriage to an infidel a daughter or sister without her knowledge and contrary to her wish.
- Canon LXIX. - Of one of the faithful who departs from the faith through lust and love of an infidel; and of the form of receiving him back, or admitting him to penance.
- Canon LXX. - Of the hospital to be established in every city, and of the choice of a superintendent and concerning his duties.
- Canon LXXI. - Of the placing a bishop or archbishop in his chair after ordination, which is enthronization.
- Canon LXXII. - No one is allowed to transfer himself to another church than that in which he was ordained; and what is to be done in the case of one cast out forcibly without any blame attaching to him.
- Canon LXXIII. - The laity shall not choose for themselves priests in the towns and villages without the authority of the chorepiscopus; nor an abbot for a monastery; and that no one should give commands as to who should be elected his successor after his death, and when this is lawful for a superior.
- Canon LXXIV. - How sisters, widows, and deaconesses should be made to keep their residence in their monasteries; and of the system of instructing them; and of the election of deaconesses, and of their duties and utility.
- Canon LXXV. - How one seeking election should not be chosen, even if of conspicuous virtue; and how the election of a layman to the aforesaid grades is not prohibited, and that those chosen should not afterward be deprived before their deaths, except on

account of crime.
- Canon LXXVI. - Of the distinctive garb and distinctive names and conversation of monks and nuns.
- Canon LXXVII. - That a bishop convicted of adultery or of other similar crime should be deposed without hope of restoration to the same grade; but shall not be excommunicated.
- Canon LXXVIII. - Of presbyters and deacons who have fallen only once into adultery, if they have never been married; and of the same when fallen as widowers, and those who have fallen, all the while having their own wives. Also of those who return to the same sin as well widowers as those having living wives; and which of these ought not to be received to penance, and which once only, and which twice.
- Canon LXXIX. - Each one of the faithful while his sin is yet not public should be mended by private exhortation and admonition; if he will not profit by this, he must be excommunicated.
- Canon LXXX. - Of the election of a procurator of the poor, and of his duties.

APPENDIX II: BIBLIOGRAPHY

Primary sources[359]

I-XIV cent.:
- Athanasius Alexandrinus, *Ad Afros Epistola Synodica*
- Athanasius Alexandrinus, *De Concilii*
- Athanasius Alexandrinus, *De Decretis*
- Athanasius Alexandrinus, *De Incarnatione Verbi Dei*
- Athanasius Alexandrinus, *Epistulae*
- Athanasius Alexandrinus, *Historia Arianorum*
- Athanasius Alexandrinus, *Oratio I Contra Arianos*
- Athanasius Alexandrinus, *Oratio II Contra Arianos*
- Athanasius Alexandrinus, *Historia Arianorum*
- Aurelius Augustinus Hipponiensis, *Confessiones*
- Aurelius Augustinus Hipponiensis, *Contra Sermonem Arianorum*
- Aurelius Augustinus Hipponiensis, *Epistolae*
- Aurelius Augustinus Hipponiensis, *De Natura et Gratiâ contra Pelagium*
- Basilius Caesarensis, *Epistulae*
- Clemens Romanus, *Epistula ad Corinthios*
- Thascius Caecilius Cyprianus, *De Laude Martyrii*
- Dionysius Exiguus, *Liber Canonum*
- Epiphanius Scholasticus, *Historia Ecclesiastica*
- Epiphanius Salamisensis, *Panarion*
- Eusebius Pamphili Caesarensis, *Historia Ecclesiastica*
- Eusebius Pamphili Caesarensis, *Vita Constantini*
- Gelasius Romanus, *Historia Concilii Nicæni*
- Gelasius Romanus, *Syntagma*
- Hieronymus Stridoniensis, *Chronicon*
- Hilarius Pictaviensis, *Contra Constantium*
- Hilarius Pictaviensis, *De Trinitate*
- Ignatius Antiocensis, *Epistola ad Ephesios*
- Ignatius Antiocensis, *Epistola ad Smyrneans*
- Iohannes Scholasticus, *Nomocanon*
- Flavius Iustinus Martys, *Apologia*
- Lucius Caecilius Firmianus Lactantius, *Epitome de Divinae Institutiones*
- Pastor Hermasii, *Similitudes*

---

[359] The order is given by the common name referred to the author

- Photius Constantinopolitanus, *Collectionem Canonum*
- Caius Plinius Caecilius Secundus, *Epistualae*
- Theodoretus Cyrrhensis, *Historia Ecclesiae*
- *Rufinus Aquileiensis*, Historia Ecclesiastica
- Socrates Scholasticus, *Historia Ecclesiae*
- Salminius Hermias Sozomenus, *Historia Ecclesiae*
- Quintus Septimius Florens Tertullianus, *De Corona Militis*

XV – XIX cent.
- AA.VVV., *The Catholic Encyclopedia*, Robert Appleton Company, 1909
- G. Aubespine, *De veteribus Ecclesiae Ritibus, Observationum Libri II*, Expensis Gregorii P. & Michaelis F. Stasi, 1770
- J. Bingham, *The Antiquities of the Christian Church*, Oxford University Press, 1855
- M.B.C. Fleury, *Histoire ecclésiastique*, Paris, Mariette, 1691-1738
- G.D. Fuchs, *Bibliothek der Kirchenver-sammlungen*, Leipsic 1780-1784
- A. Hammond, *The Definitions of Faith and Canons of Discipline of the Six Œcumenical Councils*, Oxford University Press, 1879
- Justellus, *Bibliotheca Juris Canonici*, Paris, 1661
- J.P.N. Land, *Anecdota Syriaca*, Leiden, 1889
- E.T. Merrill, *Essays in Early Christian History*, Macmillan, 1924
- E. Missing Sewell, *History of the Early Church from the First Preaching of the Gospel to the Council of Nicea*, D. Appleton and Company, 1884
- A. Neander, *Church History*, CFT Schneider, 1828
- D. Olufallidis, *Agiographies of the Most Important Saints of the Church*, Theotokos Publishing, 1879
- P. Schaff, *History of the Christian Church*, Hendrickson Publishers, 1885
- W. Smith, S. Cheetham, *Dictionary of Christian Antiquities*, John Murray, 1875
- L. Surius, *Vitae Sanctorum*, Cologne, 1617
- Z.B. Van Espen, *Tractatus Historicus Exhibens Scholia in Omnes Canones Conciliorum...*, Louvain, 1753
- Voltaire, *Philosophic Dictionary*, Paris, 1694 – 1778
- P. Westcott, *On the New Testament Canon*, MacMillan, 1855

Secondary sources:

- AA.VV., *Encyclopædia Britannica*, Britannica, 2005
- AA.VV., *The Cambridge Companion to the Age of Constantine*, Cambridge University Press, 2005

- AA.VV., *The Jordanville Orthodox Prayer Book*, Holy Trinity Monastery, 2003
- R. Algheimer, *The Council of Nicea*, Preston Press, 2001
- V. Armetrano, *L'Arco di Costantino*, Aureliana, 1991
- M.M. Arnold, *Nicaea and the Nicene Council of AD 325*, Arno Publications, 1987
- R. Attworth, *Nicea: the Council that Changed Christianity*, Best Value Publishing House, 1997
- T.D. Barnes, *The New Empire of Diocletian and Constantine*, Harvard University Press, 1982
- T.D. Barnes, *Constantine and Eusebius*, Harvard University Press, 2006
- R. Beck, *The Religion of the Mithras Cult in the Roman Empire: Mysteries of the Unconquered Sun*, Oxford University Press, 2007
- L. Berkhof, *The History of Christian Doctrines*, Banner of Truth, 1996
- A. Borman, *The Church of the First Centuries*, Alkemia, 2004
- D. Brown, *The Da Vinci Code*, Doubleday, 2003
- F.F. Bruce, *The New Testament Documents: Are They Reliable?*, IVP, 1960
- F.F. Bruce, *The Spreading Flame: The Rise and Progress of Christianity, from its First Beginnings to the Conversion of the English*, Eerdmans Publishing Co., 1979
- P.M. Bruun, *The Roman Imperial Coinage*, Spink, 2003
- J. Burckhardt, *The Age of Constantine the Great*, University of California Press, 1983
- L.H. Canfield, *The Early Persecutions Of The Christians*, Lawbook Exchange, 2005
- J. Carrol, *Constantine's Sword. The Church and the Jews: A History*, Houghton Mifflin, 2001
- W.H. Carroll, *The Revolution Against Christendom: A History of Christendom*, Christendom Press 2006
- H. Chadwick, *The Early Church*, Penguin, 1993
- B.H. Cooper, *The Free Church Of Ancient Christendom and its Subjugation Under Constantine*, Kessinger Publishing, 2006
- K. Curtis, C.P. Thiede, *From Christ to Constantine: The Trial and Testimony of the Early Church*, Christian History Institute, 1992
- R.J. DeSimone, *The Treatise of Novatian, the Roman Presbyter on the Trinity: A Study of the Text and the Doctrine*, Studia Ephemeridis "Augustinianum", 1970
- T. Dowley, *The History of Christianity*, Lion Publishing, 1990
- T. Dowley, *Introduction to the History of Christianity*, Augsburg Fortress Publishers, 1994

- G. Downey, *The Late Roman Empire*, Holt, Rinehart and Winston, 1969
- H.A. Drake, *Constantine and the Bishops: The Politics of Intolerance*, The Johns Hopkins University Press, 2002
- D. Dudley, *History of the First Council of Nice*, A & B Book Dist Inc, 2002
- A.R. Dulles, *A History of Apologetics*, Ignatius Press, 2005
- B.D. Ehrman, *Lost Christianities: The Battles for Scripture and the Faiths We Never Knew*, Oxford U.P, 2005
- E. Ferguson, *Backgrounds of Early Christianity*, Wm. B. Eerdmans Publishing Company 1993
- L. Finkelstein, *Akiba: Scholar, Saint and Martyr*, Jewish Publication Society, 1962
- T.M. Finn, *Early Christian Baptism and the Catechumenate: East and West Syria*, The Liturgical Press/Michael Glazier, 1992
- W.H.C. Frend, *The Early Church*, Fortress Press, 1985
- E. Gibbon, *The Decline and Fall of the Roman Empire*, Phoenix Press, 2005
- J.L. Gonzalez, *A History of Christian Thought*, Abingdon Press, 1970
- R.C. Gregg, *Arianism: Historical and Theological Reassessments - Papers from the Ninth International Conference on Patristic Studies*, Wipf & Stock Publishers, 2006
- H.M. Gwatkin, *The Arian Controversy*, BiblioBazaar, 2007
- J. Hannah, *Lecture Notes for the History of Doctrine*, Nav Press, 2002
- R.P.C. Hanson, *The Search for the Christian Doctrine of God: The Arian Controversy, 318-381*, Baker Academic, 2006
- W. Harrelson, R.M. Falk, *Jews and Christians: A Troubled Family*, Abingdon Press, 1990
- M. Holbourn, *Constantine the Great*, Oxford University Press, 1995
- P. Hughes, *A History of the Church*, Sheed and Ward, 1979
- A. Hunwick, *Critical Edition of Ecce Homo by Baron D'Holbach*, Mouton de Gruyter, 1995
- F.J.F. Jackson, *The History of the Christian Church to A.D. 461*, George Allen and Unwin Ltd., 1965
- L.C. Jackson, *Faith of Our Fathers: A Study of the Nicene Creed*, Canon Press, 2007
- H. Jedin, *History of the Church*, Burns & Oates, 1980
- T. Julian, *Constantine, Christianity and Constantinople*, Trafford Publishing, 2006
- D. Kagan, *The End of the Roman Empire: Decline or Transformation?*, D C Heath & Co, 1992

- J.N.D. Kelly, *Early Christian Creeds*, Longman Group Ltd., 1972
- J.N.D. Kelly, *Early Christian Doctrines*, A&C Black, 1989
- K. Kirshenhousen, *Patristic Philology*, Haberdorff, 1983
- W. Leadbetter, *Galerius and the Will of Diocletian*, Routledge, 2008
- J. Lebreton, *Heresy and Orthodoxy (A History of the Early Church)*, Collier Books, 1962
- J.C.S. Léon, *Los bagaudas: rebeldes, demonios, mártires. Revuelatas campesinas in Galia e Hispania durante el Bajo Imperio*, University of Jaén, 1996
- L. Lewys, *Constantine and the Church: Strategy of a Difficult Marriage*, Absalom 2004
- J.T. Lienhard, *The Bible, the Church, and Authority: The Canon of the Christian Bible in History and Theology*, Michael Glazier Books, 1995
- S. Lieu, *Constantine: History, Historiography and Legend*, Routledge, 1998
- W.P. Loewe, *The College Student's Introduction to Christology*, Michael Glazier Books, 1996
- R. MacMullen, *Christianizing the Roman Empire: A. D. 100-400*, Yale University Press, 1986
- E.L. Martin, *The Original Bible Restored*, ASK Publications, 1984
- V. Matthews, *A Brief History of Ancient Israel*, John Knox Press, 2002
- L.M. McDonald, *The Formation of the Christian Biblical Canon*, Hendrickson Publishers, 1995
- J. McDowell, *Da Vinci Code: A Quest for Answers*, Green Key Books, 200
- I. McGregor, *The Enemies of the Church Are my Enemies. The Roots of the Alliance Between Church and Empire*, Colton Press, 2002
- C.S. Meyer, *Moving Frontiers*, Concordia Publishing House, 1986
- B. M. Metzger, *The Canon of the New Testament: Its Origin, Development, and Significance*, Oxford University Press, 1997
- J.S. Morningdale, *The Policy of Constantine the Great Towards Christians*, Absalom, 2001
- H. Newell Bate, *Catholic and Apostolic: Collected Papers of Cuthbert Hamilton Turner*, Mowbray, 1931
- J.H. Newman, *The Arians of the Fourth Century*, Longmans Green and Co., 1909
- M. J. Nicasie, *Twilight of empire: The Roman Army from the Reign of Diocletian until the Battle of Adrianople*, J.C. Gieben, 1998
- C.M. Odahl, *Constantine and the Christian Empire*, Routledge, 2004
- J. O'Grady, *Early Christian Heresies*, New Ed edition, 1995
- I. Ortiz de Urbina, *Storia dei Concili Ecumenici*, Libreria Editrice Vaticana, 1994
- H.G. Pagetown, *Diocletian*, Harvey, 2006

- D.C. Parker, *The Living Text of the Gospels*, Cambridge University Press, 1997
- B.A. Pearson, *Ancient Gnosticism: Traditions and Literature*, Fortress Press, 2007
- D.S. Potter, *The Roman empire at Bay: AD 180–395*, Routledge 2005
- J. Prescott, *Christianity and Romanity: How Christians Conquered Rome*, Geminal, 1992
- F. and D. Radecki, *Tumultuous Times*, St. Joseph's Media, 2004
- A. Reedson, *The post-Nicean Faith*, Spencer&Co., 1991
- R. Rees, *Diocletian and the Tetrarchy*, Edinburgh University Press, 2004
- T. Roman, *The Myth of a Christian Emperor: Constantine an His links to Christianity*, Rowan Editions, 2002
- R.E. Rubenstein, *When Jesus Became God: The Struggle to Define Christianity During the Last Days of Rome*, Harvest Books 2000
- K. Rudolph, *Gnosis: The Nature and History of Gnosticism*, HarperOne, 1987
- A. Samuel, *Constatius and Constantine*, Oxford University Press, 2002
- J. Solomon, *The Growth of Christianity in the Roman Empire*, Everton Press, 1994
- M.P. Southern, *The Roman Empire from Severus to Constantine*, Routledge, 2001
- R. Stark, *The Rise of Christianity: How the Obscure, Marginal, Jesus Movement Became the Dominant Religious Force*, HarperOne 1997
- G. de Ste.Croix, M.Whitby, J.Streeter, *Christian Persecution, Martyrdom, and Orthodoxy*, Oxford University Press, 2006
- L. Strobel, *The Case for Christ*, Zondervan, 1998
- L.L. Thompson, *The Book of Revelation: Apocalypse and Empire*, Oxford University Press, 1990
- K.J. Von Hefele, *A History of the Councils of the Church, from the Original Documents*, Ams Pr Inc, 1975
- W. Walker, *A History of the Christian Church*, Scribner, 1985
- H. B. Workman, *Persecution in the Early Church*, Oxford University Press, 1906
- R.A. Whitacre, *A Patristic Reader*, Endrickson Publishers, 2007
- M. Wiles, *Archetypal Heresy: Arianism through the Centuries*, Oxford University Press, 2001
- R. Williams, *Arius: Heresy and Tradition*, Wm. B. Eerdmans Publishing Company, 2002
- S. Williams, *Diocletian and the Roman Recovery*, Routledge, 1996
- D.F. Wright, J.D. Woodbridge, *Public Faith: From Constantine to the*

Medieval World, A.D. 312-600, Baker Books, 2005
- F.J. Zrodowski, *The Concept of Heresy According to Cardinal Hosius*, The Catholic University of America Press, 1947

SPECIAL THANKS

At the end of this work all my gratitude goes to:
- God, the first Source of any inspiration and knowledge;
- my family and friends that always supported me, standing my long sessions of silence and research;
- Professor Glenn Mollette, Professor Brent Largent and all the Staff of the Newburgh Theological Seminary of Newburgh (IN.) that always helped me in my studies;
- all the ones studying these matters before, as every day I am more and more convinced that we are just "dwarves on the shoulders of giants".

A very special "thank you" to all of them!

www.ingramcontent.com/pod-product-compliance
Lightning Source LLC
Chambersburg PA
CBHW020853090426
42736CB00008B/357